I
PROMISE
YOU A
CROWN

Rekindling the Inner Fire
Devotional Series

A06

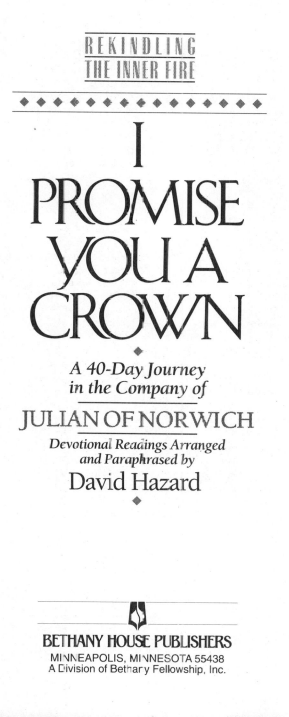

REKINDLING
THE INNER FIRE

❖ ❖ ❖ ❖ ❖ ❖ ❖ ❖ ❖ ❖ ❖ ❖ ❖

I
PROMISE
YOU A
CROWN

❖

*A 40-Day Journey
in the Company of*

JULIAN OF NORWICH

*Devotional Readings Arranged
and Paraphrased by*

David Hazard

❖

BETHANY HOUSE PUBLISHERS
MINNEAPOLIS, MINNESOTA 55438
A Division of Bethany Fellowship, Inc.

Published by Bethany House Publishers
A Ministry of Bethany Fellowship, Inc.
11300 Hampshire Avenue South
Minneapolis, Minnesota 55438

Printed in the United States of America.

Library of Congress Cataloging-in-Publication Data

Julian, of Norwich, b. 1343.
    [Revelations of divine love. English. Selections]
    I promise you a crown ; a 40-day journey in the company of Julian of Norwich : devotional readings / arranged and paraphrased by David Hazard.
        p.   cm. — (Rekindling the inner fire)

    1. Spiritual life—Catholic Church—Early works to 1800. 2. Meditations—Early works to 1800. 3. Devotional calendars. I. Title. II. Series.
BX2181.J852513   1995
242—dc20   95–7524
ISBN 1–55661–606–6   CIP

To Annie Herring,
who knows love
and who has seen Him.

Foreword

"Do not be afraid . . . be faithful . . . and I will give you the crown of life."

Revelation 2:10

*L*ittle is known about Julian of Norwich. And this is oddly fitting, because every impulse of her one written work—known as her *Revelations of Divine Love*—directs our attention away from everything that is of this earth, and of this life, to God himself. Her words, and the little we do know about Julian, tell us her faith comes from the same high and holy well as the one that poured forth visions to the Apostle John, whose sighting of God made him declare, "God is love."

For the record, this is most of what we know about Julian, who was one of the greatest Christian mystics of all time.

In 1342, somewhere in or near Norwich, England, a daughter was born to a family of humble means.

It's possible the child's real name was Julian. But it's also possible she took the name when she joined a sisterhood and began a life of contemplative prayer, living at St. Julian's Church in Norwich. The earlier Julian had forfeited her life centuries before when, for the love of Christ, she had refused to worship the Roman gods. Our Julian, for love of Christ, lived as an "anchorite," which meant she committed her entire life to focused prayer for the spread of the gospel and the salvation of the world.

Sometime in the spring of 1373, when Julian was about thirty, she fell gravely ill. Remember that plagues ravaged Europe in these, the Middle Ages. I doubt that death was delightful to these people— but on the other hand it was not the surprise and horror it is for us in the twentieth century, with our life insurances and lawsuits and illusions that we can fortress ourselves against suffering and loss. As the spring sun grew stronger, and Julian grew weaker, it appeared she was spiritually ready to move on from this life with all its physical aches and losses—on to the higher lands of heaven where she had already fixed her heart. In those days at least, earth was exile and heaven was home.

On the morning of May 13, her sisters in Christ gathered at Julian's bedside to pray beside the gray, limp figure. She was failing fast. Her hands and feet grew cold. She lost feeling. A cross hung on the wall opposite her bed, and she fixed her eyes on it. Darkness began to close—something like nausea and cold together—and numbness raced up her face. Death was taking her. With her last ounce of earthly strength, she fought to keep her eyes turned to the cross of Christ her Lord. . . .

. . . And in this perishing state, somewhere between earth and heaven, came her first vision. She saw Christ crucified, surrounded by invisible demonic horrors. She was awed by the greatness of what she saw—as she later put it, ". . . that He who is so high had come so low, for *love*." Perhaps she thought her crucified and risen Lord had come to receive her to His side in eternity.

She was not, on that May morning, so fortunate. He turned her spirit back to its earthly outpost. Her vision of Christ's amazing love came with sealed orders from on high.

Her friends were shocked when the flush of life returned to Julian's face. In moments, she was fully alive, if exhausted from the ordeal. But she was changed. An unspeakable light poured from her face. Her soul was quiet, high, serene, regal, and like a bird that can circle far above the earth.

She had come back, it seems, with an assignment. For the next forty-three years, until her quiet death in 1416, she struggled to write out all her vision had shown her about the love of God. And not the one vision only. Now that the inward eyes of her soul were opened, she was subjected to other "showings." Once the soul is opened and we know how to see beyond our *selves*, you could say, God will keep walking by.

What made Julian's writing a struggle is the

difficulty of trying to convey in completely inadequate human language a knowledge of things that comes from above. Every Christian who has had a mystical quality to his or her faith, from Augustine to Amy Carmichael, has complained about this problem.

Now, "mystical" is a frightening word for many Christians today. In one sense it is wiser to stay away from a type of spirituality that you don't understand; people get in trouble when they seek supernatural thrills. "Mysticism" is the practice of basing one's faith mainly or solely on supernatural experiences, or placing any type of supernatural experience above the authority of Scripture. This is categorically to be avoided. But strong, orthodox Christians who have sought Christ *have* sometimes had a mystical side to their faith, and we might as well face it. It was not doctrine alone that converted Augustine—it was seeing God. It was not memorizing Scripture that carried one of our greatest missionaries, Amy Carmichael, through seventeen years of hellish, crippling pain as she worked against child prostitution in India—it was her ability to see beyond the visible, into the invisible.

In any case, Julian tried to write her first account of her vision soon after she was allowed out of bed. The first draft was inadequate and she knew it. Besides that, what she saw was so like a living seed that it kept working its way deeper into her soul, giving her new insights as it grew and unfolded.

And in her meditations, further revelations came. Some twenty or thirty years after her first vision, she had to amend the whole thing. Writing and prayer occupied the rest of her adult life.

Revelations of Divine Love is considered by some to be without equal in the spiritual literature of England. It is simple, winsome, and profound. Julian was genuinely unsophisticated and uncomplicated. And yet her writing explores the deepest mysteries of the Christian faith. How can man have free will and be "predestined"? How can man be blamed for the Fall if God, who is greater, knew ahead of time he would sin? What is God's response to the suffering of innocents?

. . . I'm afraid this information, alone, is not enough to help us benefit from Julian's writings. What we'll need additionally is to step out of our modern world view and change our thinking. Two big differences separate many of us from Julian of Norwich.

First, Julian's spirituality is *God-centered* and not *man-centered.* The difference is much like the distance between earth and heaven.

Julian's God-centered faith, for starters, rests on the firm conviction that God is the prime mover, the first force behind everything. By contrast, a man-centered approach to spirituality often leaves us trying to figure out how to think, pray, behave, tithe, serve, in such a way as to get God to wake up and do things in response to our actions. To Julian,

God is always at work, and we are the ones who, blinded by our fleshly senses, need to wake up.

Along with His primal action, God is first, always, and only *good*. A later writer, Hannah Whitall Smith, would echo Julian in saying "because God is good He cannot do bad things." Therefore, He only allows evil to come into our personal lives—and He does allow it—in order to perform holy purposes. Julian doesn't try to skirt the matter of God's sovereignty, as we often do, by saying that God is the author of the nice and good things, making Satan the author of hard and painful and tempting things. God may use Satan—not to mention our own evil motives—to school us and bring us out of our imprisonment to self into Him.

So you can see why we need this higher, older perspective if we are going to understand some of her more challenging statements, such as: "The power of our Enemy is shut up in the hand of our Friend." "Sin is necessary." And her insistence that God will one day perform an act of re-creation and restitution so full of wonders that, by comparison, even the most horrible suffering of innocents will then be seen as "nothing at all."

But my real purpose in introducing the concept of God-centeredness here is this: Though Julian takes pains to give us explanations for these statements, *we all have to make the first leap of faith on our own.* Either we stand on God's side and view pain and sin and life from His higher perspective, or we stand here on our side and argue and try to make Him answer our "Why?" to the satisfaction of our rational mind. Julian's spirituality forces us to choose—to stay here on our own . . . or to make the leap.

Second, Julian's spirituality recognizes that the life of faith is a *practice.* Modern spirituality often has to do with making *moment-in-time* trips from the pew to "the altar" when we've made a mental decision—then learning to produce the right Christian "fruit," in terms of *right* behavior. Julian's spirituality involves growing in a *moment-by-moment* awareness that God is at work in everything that comes into our life—then asking for the godly wisdom, patience, and strength to respond in the Spirit and attitude of Christ. In short, her view of the spiritual life recognizes the "walk in the Spirit" as the daily practice by which God helps us to respond to Him and to our world in the character of His Son.

Here is my purpose in pointing out these distinctions: I can fool myself. I can *know* the Bible and I can *agree* with the Bible—and maybe I can *argue* a heathen or a godless intellectual into the ground with the Bible. But that will not open me to God in a way that allows the promised "rivers of living water" to flow from my inmost being. That wonderful new life from above only comes as you and I learn how to *live* in the way the Bible says we are to live. *Know* the Bible, by all means. But as the Bible says, learn how to *become* children of the living God. Live in the Way—the manner and attitude—of Jesus. To do that is a daily practice, and not a place of arrival.

This is a very freeing way to live—to follow this daily path of "putting on" Christ. Soon we begin to leave behind the old self, with all its constantly emerging tendencies toward sin, judgment, and self-righteousness. It routes us deeper into the love of God—and from that Source springs a genuine love for other men and women and inner strength for each new day.

As you begin this, the eighth REKINDLING THE INNER FIRE devotional, I pray that the Spirit of Christ will open you to a greater, sweeter, and stronger knowledge of our Father of lights. May Julian's words and attitudes challenge and comfort your spirit, too.

Mostly, I pray that you will encounter the One who promises us the crown of Life . . . today, and in the world to come!

David Hazard
May 1995

Contents

I
PROMISE
YOU A
CROWN

1
God Calls Us in Love

Thus says the LORD . . . "Call unto me, and I will answer thee, and show thee great and mighty things . . ."

Jeremiah 33:2–3, KJV

Never have I sought God for any kind of vision or special revelation. But I have often asked God earnestly, in prayer, to give me a deeper love for my Lord, Jesus Christ.

For I think every Christian soul needs to grow in heartfelt love for the One who, in His amazing love for us, willingly left heaven and became a mortal man, to live and toil in this weak flesh just like any one of us.

And though, as I say, I had never sought such a thing, He was pleased to show himself to me. . . .

During a time of contemplation, the eyes of my soul were lifted up. And I saw the crucified One. And my heart broke in its grief.

His cross was surrounded by a great, living, and ugly blackness, as if the air were filled with devils . . . but a pure light shone upon the still figure nailed to the cross . . . Christ, my Lord. . . .

And then I saw it—the warm red blood, seeping from under the crown of terrible thorns they had forced down upon His blessed head. This, His lifeblood, began to flow freely . . . in fact, as I watched, it became like a current, and a stream . . . like a river of life.

So overwhelmed was I, a loud cry of praise— *"Blessed be the Lord!"*—welled up spontaneously from within me. Now I thought my heart would crush, it was so overwhelmed with love, so filled with reverence for Him. For I was astonished by the wonder of it all. To think that He, who is so high, was also so humble. To think that He came from heaven to be near a sinful creature like me. And in that moment I was painfully aware I was just a woman, in low and fallen flesh.

I could only suppose our Lord, out of courtesy and love, had come to grant me special comfort. As if to prepare me for something. As if He knew that, in what remained of my life, I would be sorely tried in some way—perhaps even by the great powers of darkness. Though I knew such a thing could only happen by God's permission and with His protection.

But at that moment, with my eyes fixed upon my Lord—who once was slain, and who is now alive forevermore—I understood just one thing:

His ever-flowing love and His strength must become everything for me. To depend upon His strength must become my greatest rest. To live in the love of God—even at the cost of great sacrifice—must become my highest aim. My crown.

Then I knew, as I had never known in all my life before, that His blood is the only unfailing protection for every living creature from all the devils in hell . . . and from every other spiritual enemy that prowls this earth, trying to keep us from walking in the upward way of Christ, which is our high calling.

My High and Holy Father, thank you for hearing the call of my heart even before I open my mouth to cry out for you. . . . I know you call to me first. I come into your presence now to consider the wonder of your greatest answer to me . . . the wonder of your love, which I see in your Son, Jesus.

Father, help me to respond to your call of love by following in the Way of Jesus . . . though the darkness and the world, and my own soul's cowardice, tempt me to turn back. Lead me deeper into the humility and love that mark all your true children. Be my goal . . . my life . . . and my soul's crown.

2

He Is Love

*Happy is he that hath the God of Jacob for his help,
whose hope is in the Lord his God . . . [for] the* LORD
remains faithful forever . . . the LORD *sets prisoners free
. . . the* LORD *loves the righteous.*

Psalm 146:5, KJV; vv. 6–8, NIV

*W*e were made for happiness.

We were made for the serenity and bliss of heaven. . . .

But in this passing life, which we have here on earth, our fleshly senses do not perceive what our true self is, or what we are meant to be. We can only discern our true condition before God in faith. . . .

Yes, it is necessary to first understand the abysmal nature of our sin. We are a sin-ridden people who commit many evil deeds we ought to forsake. We leave undone many good things the Lord of Love would direct us to do.

Yet, even though we deserve pain, accusation, and anger, I saw that the Lord is truly never angry and never will be angry with us. Because He is God, He is goodness itself. He is truth. He is peace. *He is love eternal.* Therefore all His attributes—His holy power, the light of His wisdom—are united into one in His flaming love.

So I tell you that, for us who believe, God is the fiery radiance of a goodness which cannot be angry. For in His substance, God is nothing but good. Do you see what this means?

Our soul was created to be one with Him who is an outpouring of unchanging and unfailing goodness . . . united so that nothing at all can wedge in between our soul and God.

. . . God wishes for us to seek Him in this aspect of himself, which is *love without end* . . . for God showed me that in His love there are many hidden mysteries. And He will not reveal them all to us until the time when He, in His goodness, has made us ready and worthy to see them.

That is well with me. And I am satisfied as I wait upon our Lord to complete His will in this marvel—to wait and rest in the ever-unfolding wonder of His eternal Life, which even now is like a seed growing in me.

My Father, you know I get frustrated, anxious, or angry when I cannot have the things I think I need.

Draw me into the flame of your Self . . . so that your pure radiance fills me . . . and I want nothing more than you . . . nothing besides you . . . today.

3

He Searches for His Lost

He [will] come forth [who] is to be [your] ruler . . .
whose goings forth have been from of old,
from everlasting.

———

Micah 5:2, KJV

You see, at just the right time, when we were still
powerless, Christ died for the ungodly . . . if, when we
were God's enemies, we were reconciled to him through
the death of his Son, how much more . . . shall we be
saved through his life!

———

Romans 5:6, 10

The Lord was also pleased to show me a
mystery . . . a wonder of His love. . . .

I saw a stately lord, seated in his regal chambers. Before
him stood a lowly manservant—not directly in front, but to
the left—respectful and waiting to do his lord's will. The

servant waited for a long, long time, and it was clear he felt nothing but love for his lord. For I could see he was eager and straining to be sent to do a certain thing in his master's service. . . .

Oddly, the servant was dressed in clothes that were scanty and worn almost to rags, filthy with grime and sweat. And though these were his clothes, I somehow knew he had never been sent out of his lord's presence to do such hard labor. I was puzzled, for it looked as if his clothes were so thin they were about to tear or disintegrate and fall from his body.

I was thinking, "These clothes are not fitting for a servant who is so loved by his lord." For I could also see there was nothing but pleasure and joy in the eyes of the master as he looked at his manservant.

Then I was given to know that the servant had perceived the heart of his lord—that is, there was a certain high task to perform that would bring greatest honor to his lord. . . . He stood before his lord, then, and the eagerness of his whole being cried out, "How long, my lord? How long must I wait to perform your will?"

Now the lord is the blessed Father. And the servant is His Son, Jesus Christ. The task was the rescue of Adam, which is every one of us. Because of the true union made in heaven, the Son could not be separated from us, for we were made for Him. . . .

The ragged clothing I saw is our poor, weak, and aging flesh, which Christ took upon himself in order to come and to serve us in our sin. So the Son stood before His Lord—to the side, which is our rightful place—saying, "My dear Father, I stand before you clothed in Adam's flesh, ready to rush to do your will. I want to be on earth to your glory, when it is your will to send me. How long shall I wait?"—Though truly, the Son knew the Father's will, and how long he must wait, for He is the Word and Wisdom of the Father. . . .

And then the lord leaned forward and spoke something quietly, privately, to the servant. And the servant rushed out from the lord's presence as fast as He could run. . . .

The rushing out of the servant shows us the outbursting love of the Father, the swiftness with which He came to our assistance in Christ, at the perfect time . . . rushing to us as He does even now, when He knows the time is right.

My Father, there is one thing that keeps me from seeing you—and that is my fallen understanding. I don't understand why you delay when I ask for help . . . or when the kind of answer I want doesn't come at all.

Heal my mind, Lord, so I can begin to rest in knowing you and your higher ways. Help me to understand that, from of old, you have planned to come . . . not to give me answers or blessings . . . but to fill me with your life.

Teach me your ways, beginning with a new knowledge of your eager love for me.

4

He Values Us

*The devil took [Jesus] to a very high mountain and
showed him all the kingdoms of the world and their
splendor. "All this I will give you," he said, "if you will
bow down and worship me." Jesus said to him, "Away
from me, Satan! For it is written: 'Worship the Lord
your God, and serve him only.' "*

Matthew 4:8–10

*H*ow is it possible to explain something that is
only "seen" by the spirit? This has been my
struggle for many years—to explain how one "sees"
with the eyes of the soul. I cannot take up an
explanation for it now, for it is a subject all in itself.
And for now I want to tell you what I have learned
about God and how we receive His love. . . .

Once I saw the Lord Jesus—in His eager love for
us, and in His humble obedience to God—I found
myself pondering the deep, deep love of God. In
some ways, it felt like the kind of love you have for
people in your family. But it was more than that. It
was a great benevolence, a power and force that

cannot be stopped by anything.

And though I had been a Christian for some time, it was the first time I knew beyond all doubt that God is our one help, and our only real help. In God, there is only good. And only good comes to us from Him, when we are in Christ.

Immediately, my soul was tempted to turn from this view of God. I looked away from Him and started to think of all the pain and evil in the world. Immediately, I felt confused again and in conflict. How can we worship Him as a God of love, with so much wrong in the world—and so many things that hurt us, or tempt us?

I know God heard my confusion, as if it were a prayer. Because, as I muddled on these things, a sudden *knowing* arose in me. It came as I thought on the words "in Christ". . . .

I saw that Jesus—that is, His *attitude*—must become our spiritual clothing. He clothed himself in our flesh. And we must clothe ourselves in His attitude toward God—an attitude of childlike trust and complete abandon to a good Father. In this way, the love of God becomes a spiritual garment that wraps around our inner being. For we come to see—dimly at first, then more clearly—how His love embraces, watches over, protects, surrounds, shapes, and directs. We know He will never leave us alone—nor has He left us alone—no matter what it may look like from a human standpoint.

I saw that, in this attitude and mind of Christ, I must take on the new mind of *faith*, which teaches me this: In Christ, all that is good comes down to me from the hand of the Father.

For a time, I sat there, overwhelmed. A voice inside was tempting me to give up these "foolish" thoughts. *Who are you to think God loves you like this, sinful, small, and foolish person that you are? And how can you believe such nonsense when there is evil? . . . Remember the evil. . . .*

I was becoming unsettled. Confused. Dismayed.

I believe it was then the Lord showed me a small, curious thing. An object no bigger than, say, a hazelnut—small enough to lie almost unnoticed in the palm of your hand. So insignificant. As I wondered what it could be, I was given to know:

What you see is everything that is made—all of the visible creation, which seems so substantial in nature to human eyes. Look at it. For in comparison to the eternal nature of God, and in comparison to the love of God, it is so small.

I was puzzled that a thing so little could be of any importance to our great God—amazed that such a tiny thing could last. For it looked so insignificant, and like it could crumble into nothing. And again, my puzzling was answered:

This fragile creation lasts, and will ever last, only because God made it and He loves it. Only through the love of God does the substance of creation hold together and have its being. (See Colossians 1:16–17.)

As I meditated on this, an eternity of peace and rest came. This is the simple truth: *God made all of creation. He loves everything He created. By His own hand, He preserves it all.*

Selfish creature that I am, I wondered: *What is this to me?*

Again, I was given to know.

As never before, I understood. *God is the Creator, the Lover, and the Protector.* This knowledge must grow in the substance of my soul. It must replace my fear and unbelief—my foolish thought that some things are too difficult even for God to change. I must rest in the knowledge of His greatness and love until I am wholly united with Him in my very being. For if any part of my inner being is "outside" of this attitude of Christ, I can never walk in the spiritual blessings of love, or serene inward rest, or happiness.

Though I had been a Christian so long, I finally saw that the one single aim of my spirit must be this: to become so attached to my Lord that nothing in all creation can come between God and me. (See Romans 8.)

But I wondered, *Who can heal my low and sin-blinded soul so that I can reach so lofty a goal—this full trust in the goodness of God?*

Only the Lord himself. He is *able* to heal us and lift us to such heights in His Spirit. And He *will* lift us up by His mercy when the deceptions of Satan and this world cause us to fall and we are broken. And He *will* fill us and crown us with His empowering grace. This is not a spiritual life we must hope and long for only. This is the purpose for which we were created—to enjoy the life in His Spirit, which He came to restore to us. . . .

I tell you this, a secret you must know if you are a man or woman who longs to draw this spiritual life from the wells of our salvation. Though it goes against all that your fleshly lower nature will tell you, learn to count as *nothing* everything that is created and the pain or opposition that comes to you. For those who are occupied only with earthly business—those who think their security lies in earthly well-being—will never find freedom from turmoil. Neither will we if we ascribe such power to the kingdom of this world. For it is not possible that there is any power to give life or security to our souls in something that is, in its essence, so small and fleeting. . . .

Seek the crown of your life in Christ, then. By that I mean, seek to know only the love and compassion that comes down from uncreated God. For His love is the highest, and it reigns over all.

$\mathcal{M}$ighty Father, Maker and Owner of all, open my eyes today to the splendor of you . . . to all the goodness and love that spills from your heart, as from a high mountain spring. Cause the roots of my soul—my affections—to sink into the sweet, fresh waters of your Spirit . . .

. . . until I am sunk to my knees before you . . . in love with you alone.

5

He Sets Us Free

We rejoice in our sufferings, because we know that suffering produces perseverance . . . character . . . and hope. And hope does not disappoint us, because God has poured out his love into our hearts by the Holy Spirit. . . . Since we have now been justified by [Christ's] blood, how much more will we be saved . . . through him . . . [and] so we rejoice in God.

Romans 5:3–5, 9, 11 (emphasis added)

God has created plentiful waters, which flow throughout the earth for our comfort and pleasure. He did this for us because He is a Father of love, who finds happiness in blessing His children.

It is much more pleasing to Him, though, that we find freedom for our souls . . . that we know we are washed and cleansed in His blood, for it was freely poured out. . . .

I was meditating on this once, when a voice without words spoke within my soul: *By this is the Enemy overcome.*

I knew of course this referred to the Passion of our Lord, in which He was caused to spill His own blood.

It was as if I could see a picture of Satan's evil fury in which He contrived to bring the Lord of Heaven to His death on the cross. And all in a moment, I understood how frustrating it was to the fiend to realize—too late—the wicked stratagem by which he hoped to defeat God was the very thing that would bring his own final downfall . . . that is, *the shedding of God's blood!*

Then I believe the Lord was pleased to show me something else, as a clear warning. The devil's malice is just as great now as it was before the Incarnation. And this jealous anger causes him to work very hard against us, for he cannot bear the sight of so many souls escaping from him to share in the glory of God which he has lost.

And this is the thing that infuriates him most: We can rest in our spirits, knowing we are loved by God no matter what. All because He has given us everything when He poured out His blood. If we are driven to greater rest in God—that is, if we do not choose to turn away when He permits the devil to do his worst to us—then Satan's evil works do more glory for us and more anguish for him. We win a great victory in soul, and he loses.

Satan can never work as much evil as he would wish. For all the power of our Enemy is locked up in the hands of our Friend

The Lord has nothing but scorn for every bit of

the devil's puny fury—great and terrible as that fury may seem to us. God looks upon the devil, and his workings too, as insignificant. *Nothing*. And our Father wants us to take on this attitude—the mind of Christ—that anything Satan might appear to take from us for the season of this life is very small compared to the greater joy of knowing God in the Holy Spirit of Christ. (See Philippians 2–3.)

When I saw how the Lord's utter goodness thwarts all the evils of which I had once been afraid—sickness and pain, loss, betrayal and abuse at the hands of others, even death—I began to laugh. . . .

I could not stop, but laughed heartily, feeling my whole soul evermore lifted and freed from sadness and fear. . . . I wish every Christian could see by means of the Holy Spirit, and understand what I saw about the greatness of God and the smallness of every evil—no matter how terrible it appears to our weak flesh.

I must tell you, though. While I was laughing—experiencing the eternal, unstoppable joy of the Father—I did not perceive that Christ was laughing. For He is our brother in flesh, and His compassion will never allow Him to make light of our suffering while we are here. And neither should we, as His brothers and sisters, treat lightly the pain or temptation of another.

Even so, I know Jesus wants us to laugh and rejoice in God that Satan *is* overcome. For holy joy—when it is of God and not of human silliness—

brings good comfort and refreshing lightness to our spirits.

Father of happiness and laughter, when I am tempted . . . opposed . . . tried . . . open my eyes in the Holy Spirit. Let me see you as the Most High. Give me the mighty joy that is in you . . . to silence the tempting voice and overcome the evil one . . . in all his threatening disguises.

6

He Calls Us
"Friends"

[Jesus said,] "You are my friends if you do what I command. . . . You did not choose me, but I chose you to go and bear fruit—fruit that will last. . . . This is my command: Love each other."

John 15:14, 16–17

Y̶ou and I must not place ourselves at the center of all things. By that I mean we must not measure everything by how it affects us—judging other people according to our standards, criticizing their actions because they do not make sense to us. Instead, we must remain as one, in *love* with every brother and sister in Christ.

If I pay special attention to myself, then I am nothing at all.

If I claim to be saved, then my life will consist in this—I will be growing daily in the unity of love with all other Christians.

I tell you this: If anyone withdraws his love

from any of his fellow Christians, it shows he is walking outside of the love of God. For as I have said, God created all, and He loves all. Moreover, if you refuse to love someone—for the love of God comes from the will, not from our emotions—you put yourself in danger. For then you are living apart from God's will, which is the offer of peace to all men. (See Luke 2:14.)

If I love, as God loves, I am safe. . . . And the more I choose to love with God's love while I am here on earth, the more I am changed. That is, the more I love, the more I become like light and blessedness itself—like the luminous bliss I will step into one day when I pass from this place into the world that is eternal.

God is joy and love without end. Was this not the gift He offered us, when He chose to step out of eternity, and to come down into this world to be our brother?

. . . I know it is love that moves me to tell you these things. For I want the beauty of God to be known. And I want my brothers and sisters in Christ to prosper in spirit—just as I long to grow in Christ—by hating the sin of self-centeredness that divides and hurts us. This we can conquer by loving God more.

My Father—Father of all—there are people I dislike . . . people I find dull or irritating. . . . And there are people I favor because of appearance, money, position, or talents. People I favor because they think like me. . . .

Is it possible that what I call love is really something else—only a form of self-centeredness?

As you humbled yourself, humble me. I want to become your true friend. Send me, today, "down" from the heights of my opinion, comfort, and self-centered preference. And send to me, whoever you want me to love.

7

He Gives Us Goodness

How many are your works, O LORD! In wisdom you made them all. . . . When you open your hand, [we] are satisfied with good things. When you hide your face, [we] are terrified.

Psalm 104:24, 28–29

*T*here was a day when the Lord sent into my soul one of the highest moments of delight I had ever known. It was like an unknown taste, or a fragrance—exquisite and rare. My soul was lifted.

But the moment was so fleeting. In a breath it was gone. Yet I was filled completely with a sense that remained in me far longer—a solid assurance about life everlasting. It was as strong as an anchor to my soul, so that I felt secure forever and forever.

I cannot say this strongly enough. This security was like finding a happy welcome within the great walls of a rich fortress. In that moment, I was entirely at ease, at rest, and I knew that nothing on this earth could ever harm me again. I enjoyed this peace for some time. . . .

And then all was changed. In a flicker of time, I was suddenly left to myself, as one abandoned in a terrible wilderness. Oppression, isolation, rolled over me . . . on and on. Soon, I was despairing of my life. I could not imagine where I would find the strength to endure and go on living for even a little while longer.

What was worse, I knew the only thing that could ease my pains of lonely torment were these things—the *hope* that spills down to us by the grace of God, the *faith* He sheds on us so that our spirits may be opened to perceive Him, and the *love* that surrounds and sustains us all.

But in that instant I was bereft of every shred of these true graces.

. . . Then, once again, the peaceful security came flooding back, the rest that comes only in knowing your soul is hidden in God. Again, I knew myself to be surrounded in the light of His blessing. The sense of it was so vast—above, below, and all around me, magnificent as an ocean. And fear, sorrow, physical agony, spiritual torment—all these terrible things seemed to be breaking around me, but at a great distance. For I was being carried, gently and undisturbed, in these, the depths of God.

Many times these two extremes of spirit flooded through me. Abysmal emptiness. Joy, fair enough to crush the soul. Back and forth. Again and again.

In the swells of joy, I could have shouted along with the Apostle Paul—"*Nothing can separate me from the love of God that is in Christ Jesus my Lord!*" And during the dark trenches of anguish, I wanted to shout out with Peter—"*Lord, save me! I am dying!*"

And when it was all through, I was at quiet rest within myself, with a *certain knowledge* that was newly alive inside me. It was this:

The Father knows every man and woman *needs* to go through times like these. Times when we feel His comfort, and times when we feel utterly abandoned. He wants us all to know that—no matter how it *seems*—He keeps us safe all the time, in happiness and misery. His love is ever as strong, in both sorrow and celebration.

Moreover, there are times when the Father knows that leaving us to feel we are on our own will strengthen our soul. We should never think, when we feel abandoned by Him, it is because we have sinned—for, in fact, when we agonize because we have fallen into sin, He is most willing to come to us with His forgiveness and strengthening grace. . . .

I tell you again, God sends us showers of happiness freely. And sometimes, for our soul's profit, He sends sorrow. *Both come from His love.*

Above all, do everything you can to preserve—even if only in memory—the times of comfort that come to you from God. For the pain of this life is passing and soon will be reduced to dust, and it will vanish. But the joy that comes down from heaven—*that* is a taste of the eternal, and even the taste lasts forever!

It is never God's will that we should spend our days chasing after sadness and grief, great as they seem to our fallen soul without the eyes of faith. May He show you, as He showed me, how to leave such truly small things behind. . . .

My Father, you who live outside of time, I know you sometimes perform your "dark" work. I know you hide yourself so I will leave behind all that occupies my strength and attention to seek you again.

In everything, Lord, draw me straight to your heart. Help me to move beyond this life's inevitable losses and hurts.

8

He Holds Us Close

Jesus said, "Let the little children come to me. . . ."
And he took the children in his arms. . . .

Mark 10:14, 16 *(emphasis added)*

*E*verything that is *beneath* God, everything that is *less than* God, is not good enough for us.

And God, our Father, wants every one of us, His children, to know this.

For this reason, the soul has no rest until it can stand above every created thing. For nothing made can compare with uncreated God. We must fight to possess this truth because our inner man will always want to find security in things of this world.

I shall tell you a secret of spiritual strength:

Learn how to oppose your own will. Begin to still the voice of your soul—which is your will—so that your inner man becomes as nothing. You must do so in order to see yourself within God's all-surrounding love. This is a great struggle, a fight to the death to win the ground of your soul. But when it is accomplished you will have Him who is everything. You will have won your soul, and your soul will have received rest.

This can only be done if the eyes of your faith are opened to the complete goodness of the Father. As His child, remind your soul of His goodness—even in what appears to be the most terrible times of pressure and opposition. The reminder of His complete goodness will be sweetness to your soul. You will remain so close to Him, in your spirit and will, that you can nearly feel His touch.

God's goodness *does* fill all of His creatures, and everything that is the work of His hands. He longs to fill them so full that they overflow like springs, issuing in endless streams of His goodness. How can it be otherwise? For God is everlasting, from everlasting. He made us to be His alone, with no part of us owing higher allegiance to anything less than himself. He brought us back to himself by the breaking of His own human body. (See Colossians 1:20–23.) Having given himself for us, why would He now become slack in any way, or fail to issue streams of goodness and love for His children's souls to drink from?

I was shown this, I believe, in order to help others look upon life with the eyes of wisdom, and not with fleshly eyes only. If you are wise, you will cling to the goodness of God.

From this, you may also draw a bit of instruction about your prayers. Many Christians remain in blindness on these matters, and when something happens to make them uncomfortable in the least, they run from one person to another. They seek many opinions, many prayers—as if God is so hardhearted He will not bend down to lift the weakest of His children to himself.

When we come to Him in prayer, we should begin as one who has come to the highest place a soul may reach—to God himself. We must see ourselves as standing at the wellspring of ever-flowing goodness! It is so honoring to God to come to Him in prayer, declaring His goodness over all. And it brings so much sweetness to the soul. So many miss this, and it is the *true beginning of prayer*.

Come to Him, then, and start your prayers by resting quietly and completely in His goodness. You will quickly find this inner rest is the very thing that makes it possible for Him to flood us with the power of grace—pouring himself into us . . . and out to others through us.

Enlist the prayers of as many others as you like. But no *amount* of prayer can accomplish what this beginning in simple childlike rest can do for your soul. You will find sweet refreshment that others never find. And as I said, it brings highest honor to our good Father. He only wants us to learn how to cease our struggling, and to live as if we really do trust in His goodness. . . .

My Good Father, I come to you now, and all I want is to stand in your great presence . . . to know the touch and blessing of your hands.

9
He Longs for Us

Jesus cried out, "When a man believes in me, he does not believe in me only, but in the one who sent me. When he looks at me, he sees the one who sent me. I have come into this world as a light. . . . Remain in me, and I will remain in you. . . ."

John 12:44–46; 15:4

*B*e sure of this: We need the very life of God to enwrap us more closely than our own clothing. Our flesh and earthly belongings will waste away and be no more. And so they can never be enough to clothe the soul, which is eternal. But if we are clothed in the living goodness of God we lack nothing.

Of all the things we can fix our innermost thoughts upon, this truth brings most benefit to us: *God is good, and His goodness flows from a life without end.* Dwell on this truth, I say, because our Lover wants us to cleave to Him with every bit of strength we possess. Cling to Him as branches to a vine. Draw deeply from His living goodness.

Do you know, beyond all doubt, that you are God's own child and you are loved by Him without measure? It is true. Your soul is loved, with a love so tender, by the One who is highest of all. His is a love so wonderful, far beyond anything we created beings can fully fathom.

No one, in this life, can know how passionately the Creator longs for us. Enter into this love, then, by His empowering grace. Be diligent as you go to prayer. Still the nagging, worrying voices that tell you to doubt your Lover's complete trustworthiness—and fix your thoughts on His good, lofty, and limitless compassion—so that you remain in His love. *Trust Him.*

Learn what it means to hide your soul in Him in this way, in utter trust. After that, your prayers will be filled with true reverence—that is, a joyful respect not mixed with resentment, demands, or bargaining. For then our natural will is to have God *himself*—nothing less. And God's good will is simply to have *us*. To wrap us in himself, and in eternal life.

Never stop willing or loving, until you are united with Him in happy completeness. . . .

This is the sturdy foundation on which everything else in your spiritual life depends, now and forever.

My Father, when life feels dark, tasteless, and dry—is it because my soul has gone too long without the touch and taste of your life within me?

Today, I will not look to this world or anyone in it as the source of my love and security. I will bring all that concerns me and lay it in your hands, in the same trusting and open spirit of my Lord and brother, Christ. Be the Life of my life!

10

He Gives Us Honor

[Jesus said,] "I no longer call you servants, because a servant does not know his master's business. Instead, I have called you friends, for everything that I have learned from my Father I have made known to you."

John 15:15

The greatest honor a king can offer to one of his common workingmen is to accept him as a friend, to treat him as an equal. More than that, suppose this king makes it known to everyone— and even announces in public—"This is my closest friend."

The man would think, *What higher honor could the king give me than this? Medals and awards really don't compare to the honor and respect that come when people know you are the close friend of a king. Even an expensive gift wouldn't amount to very much if the king still kept me at a distance and treated me as if I were beneath him.*

I tell you this, of course, because this is exactly

how it is between the Lord Jesus and ourselves. What other happiness can lift your soul so much as this—to know that He who is highest, fairest, noblest, and most honored is also the lowest and humblest? He is so full of regal courtesy toward us, whom He accepts as brothers and sisters!

You may rest your soul on this marvelous truth: Though we must accept His graciousness by faith now, while we are in these bodies, one day we will be completely changed when we see how humbly He loves us—on the day when we see Him face-to-face!

For now, our good Lord wants us to simply believe we are accepted and welcomed by Him in this way. His acceptance is one of the graces that flows down from God, and He means for us to trust in it as a sure stream that will not fail. In fact, He sends this grace in order that we may drink from it as from streams of rejoicing and inner strength.

To think on these things will always provide unfailing waters to the soul, refreshing us until the day we see His hands stretched to us in welcome—and we *shall* see them one day, with eyes that have been made new.

May the Lord now open the eyes of your soul to this knowledge that is too wonderful to say in mere words. . . .

Humble Father, I come now, thankful and awed that you honor me with your friendship. Make me a true and good and loving friend to everyone you have sent into my life.

11
He Guides
Our Way

*Where has your lover gone? Which way did your
lover turn? . . . Come, my beloved, let us go. . . .*

Song of Songs 6:1, NIV; 7:11, KJV

*I*f God wants you to know Him in a truer way,
He will create the circumstances that drive you to
seek Him more deeply.

He creates the path. And then He is the light of
understanding that shines within you. All you need
as your guide is Him, in His person and presence.

For many years I had sought God and had seen
something of Him. But at first I was so foolish. I did
not understand that I could not even seek God
unless He himself drew me. He does so in His own
timing, for His own purposes. It is God who moves
upon us, to show us a new aspect of himself when
He needs for us to know more about Him. He does
this so we can take part in some aspect of His
greater plan, not for our mere enjoyment. Certainly

not to glorify our proud flesh, which is what happens when we think we have been given "higher" knowledge of Him than others! Therefore, it is one of His graces—to show aspects of His manifold nature to us. His silent voice is the grace that stirs us with the desire to seek Him . . . and His gift of grace is the new burst of life that lifts our soul when we have found Him.

So our inner life moves and is kept on the path of the Spirit. And we remain on this path by pursuing these sayings, both of which are true:

I saw Him—yet the more I saw the more I needed to see.

I had Him—and the more I had of Him the more I knew I lacked.

This describes the way we pursue God in this life. It is the way we keep ourselves alert to the life of the Spirit within us. We know to *rest* when He is pleased to leave us at rest in what we have known of Him so far. And we remain alert to *move on* and find Him in a greater way when He is pleased to call us to go further on with Him. Remember, He will always call us to go further than we have gone before. . . .

God's will is that we "see" Him continually, and that we understand what He is about in our lives. He may leave us at rest for a time. And then He stirs our circumstances in order to move us on into greater trust. All the while He works to remove the veil of doubt from these eyes of flesh. Every step of the way He is so kind and patient, knowing that we are groping and unsure, like the partially blind.

And as I have just told you, He wants us to live with hope and expectancy, believing He is going to reveal himself to us more and more. For God wants to be seen. And He wants us to seek. And He moves closer to us when we are expectant of His coming.

My Father, how blind and deaf I am—to miss your voice as you speak within my own being! You call to me in my restlessness and discontent. You guide me by my own confusions . . . out of my self into you.

Keep me faithful while I grope my way along—as one who searches blindly along a wall—until I understand that there is a door . . . always open. And the door is you.

12
He Opens Our Eyes

Grace was given us in Christ Jesus before the beginning of time, but it has now been revealed through the appearing of our Savior . . . who has destroyed death and has brought [our] life and immortality to light. . . .

2 Timothy 1:9–10

I was meditating on the crucifixion of Christ our Lord—and suddenly I became aware, not only of His Passion, but a sense of vileness all around. I was almost frightened at the hatred directed at Jesus. The contempt that caused evil and vulgar men to spit on His weak body. The rage that drove them to beat Him and pound nails into His flesh.

It was almost as if I could feel His pains. They were more than I can tell. . . . My spirit was quite disturbed as I contemplated the brutality and scorn our Lord went through . . . for me and for you.

God granted me an insight through this meditation.

The Lord wants us to understand the foul death we deserved to die because of our evil rebellion against Him. And also to understand the desire to save us that caused our blessed Lord to leave the brightness of heaven in order to bear the penalty for our sins—the penalty of dying a terrible death, in torment and forsaken by the Father. . . .

I can hardly tell you, as I recall the meditation now, the sorrow that discolored the face of Jesus. That most beautiful of faces! Fairest of heaven, more lovely than any flower on earth. . . .

By God's grace, I also understood something else about Him . . . something I saw in the marred beauty of our Lord.

The Father, Son, and Holy Spirit created mankind in their own wonderful image and likeness. When we fell so deeply into blindness and misery because of sin, there was only one way to restore us. And so He who created us for love— who created us *because* of love—set out to restore us to the same state of fellowship and beauty we had lost. And in truth He set out to give us even more than what we lost. . . .

So began His mission, to remake us into His image. And it is only His mighty power that can re-create the fallen soul. . . . Our Lord Jesus wanted— out of love, and for our honor—to make himself as much like us as possible. So He became like us in this mortal state, in our uncleanness and human misery—as much as He could, that is, without sinning himself. *How is it possible that God's love is so* great He could stand to conceal sublime Godhood within corrupted flesh? And yet He did so, in order that we might leave behind mortal corruption and be remade in the image of God.

Does this not tell you something about our Lord Jesus and His nature? Don't you see that no man who ever lived was as beautiful in spirit as He is?

Father of Beauty, how great is your creative power! Give me eyes to recognize every "tool" in your hands as you work to reshape me in the immortal image of your Son . . . all the words and people and circumstances that gouge, as well as those that smooth.

I trust you, Father. Shape in me the beauty of a life set apart for you.

13
He Rules in Our Weakness

*I pray also that the eyes of your heart may be
enlightened in order that you may know the hope to
which [the Lord Jesus] has called you, the riches of his
glorious inheritance in the saints, and his incomparably
great power for us who believe. . . . [For] God has placed
all things under his feet. . . .*

Ephesians 1:18–19, 22

*Who shall separate us from the love of Christ? Shall
trouble or hardship or persecution or famine or
nakedness or danger or sword?*

Romans 8:35

In a time of great physical pain, accompanied
by inward turmoil . . . I was again contemplating
Jesus and His suffering for us on the cross. I was
thinking that, while the eyes of my soul are set

upon the work of the cross, I am safe from wandering into sin. I am secure in the fortress of Christ and His saving nature.

I also saw that it is possible to let my soul look away from the cross. Then I wander outside the nature of Christ. If I would be so forgetful—or willingly foolish—then I would be sending my soul out into danger. For outside of Christ, we are venturing down into the lower darkness of the flesh. There the devils are waiting to reign over us. With this thought came a bolt of fear.

And then, gently, there came a voice within me. It would be more accurate to say a suggestion formed in my mind: *Stop looking at the cross, and look up to heaven where the Father dwells.*

By this, I understood the voice was telling me I should refuse to accept my earthly trials. As if I could be done with trials once and for all—as if it were possible to pass from the blindness and "death" of this present life and experience the full blessings of the eternal realm *now*.

Somehow I knew I was being asked to make a choice, and it was this: to experience the warfare of this life—which is our cross—or attempt to seize the blessed life that only belongs to those who have already passed above into the realm where there is no sorrow or pain. Still, I hesitated.

The voice within was now urging me to look up, or else to give an answer for my resistance.

It was then that faith arose in me—the same faith that led me to place my soul in Christ. At that moment it was as if clear light arose to shine upon my path. I knew what I must choose.

Yet a great struggle continued in me. And it took all the strength I could gather to make my choice and answer. "No," I said, "I cannot look beyond the cross, to exchange its mighty power for all the blessings of heaven. I cannot, Lord Christ, because *you* are my heaven." It had come to me that nothing can keep us from knowing the joy of heaven while we remain under the cross—that is, in humble obedience to God no matter what is sent to us.

You may wonder at this choice, and so I will tell you what faith showed me in its light.

In my struggle, I saw the terror that lies in forsaking the power of the cross. For in making our soul submit, as Jesus submitted, we are remade into the image of Christ. This will never happen if we seek only earthly blessings. When I understood this, I did not want to look up, as if I had already achieved a place in heaven among the blessed. I knew that to do so would make my soul proud and arrogant in itself.

And so I made my choice.

And I can tell you this: I would rather have remained in my terrible pain until the Day of Judgment than to try to come into heaven by any other means than the Way of Jesus. The light of faith had shown me He had bound this bundle of suffering to me. And faith showed me He would unbind me when suffering had done the work of

His will in perfecting me, whether in this life or in the life to come.

This is how I was taught that Jesus is my heaven. . . . No other heaven could attract me from Him, and He himself will be the wellspring of all my joy when I am raised to stand before His throne.

Had I known this earlier, I never would have prayed to be released from my suffering, even when it was at its worst. For when we resist suffering it is only because of the reluctance and domination of the flesh. And though we may feel every reluctance to embrace our suffering, that is only because of the weak outward man, who must come under the rulership of Christ.

Yes, you and I must make Him our Sovereign Ruler. The power and the choice lie with us. *For the power to choose submission to God belongs to the spirit within us. This is our spiritual walk in Christ.*

Since the time He made this clear to me, this has always been the comfort of my soul—to choose Jesus, in His wonderfully patient and submissive nature. This is my heaven, in every pain and sadness. Slowly it has become clearer that, in times of well-being or in trials, I must draw my entire being into total abandonment and complete submission to the good will of the Father. For that is what Christ did. I have learned that every pain and every woe is like the tender tap of the Good Shepherd's staff, directing my soul back into the Way of Life. . . .

In this world, the flesh will always experience pleasure and suffering, happiness and grief. We must never confuse the life of the flesh with the life of the spirit, though. In the innermost place of the soul we can be lifted to the side of Christ by accepting our own cross—for He longs for us to sit enthroned beside Him in His sanctuary. This sanctuary is within us. It is the most powerful position from which our benevolent Sovereign can govern our lives.

This is the inward field of battle where you must wage war in order to grow in faith—it is the place where you must choose the humility of Jesus above all else. Then He will show you all the depth, beauty, truth. and love that are contained in His nature.

Choose Him to be your heaven.

It is the only wise choice.

My Father, Keeper of the sanctuary of my soul—my heart is your altar. . . . Let your fire fall! Let your glory fill this sacred place—the glory that was revealed in the humility of your Son! . . . Come what may, make me faithful. . . .

14
He Gives Perfect Gifts

I will speak of the glorious honor of thy majesty, and of thy wondrous works. . . . The Lord is gracious and full of compassion. . . . The Lord is good to all. . . . The Lord is righteous in all his ways, and holy in all his works.

Psalm 145:5, 8–9, 17, KJV

It is God's will that we receive from Him three marvelous gifts. These will aid us on our way as we grow in Christ, so that His image radiates more and more from our innermost core.

The first gift is *diligence*—that we may stay on the spiritual path that is the Way of Christ. For we cannot deliberately, slothfully wallow in our fleshliness one day and expect to rise and progress in Christ the next—seeing that our secret inner motive is to give as much place to our flesh as possible. May the gift of steady diligence flow into your soul from the fountain of graces, and may it come with the force of the sweet joy of heaven.

Then when trouble comes you will not sink into unreasonable depression or useless sorrow.

The second is the gift of *patient endurance*. For by this gift are you given the willpower to wait for the Lord to reveal His goodness in all things, no matter how terrible circumstances may look from your human viewpoint. When you love someone, do you not thrust aside all doubt and trust that they meant you no harm, even when their motives seem unclear? We must give God the benefit of the doubt, too. And it is the gift of patient endurance that frees us from all murmuring and from resisting His will—mules that we are. Remember always that His reasons for every pain and every so-called "unanswered prayer" will be revealed to us one day, and that in view of eternity this life with its struggles is short indeed.

Patient endurance makes possible the third gift God wants to give us, which is the *eyes of faith*—by which I mean the ability to see Him going about His great work in all things. Only as we gain this spiritual vision can we come to discern Him and trust Him in all things.

God wants us to know He *will* appear, suddenly and with joy that overrides all else . . . and this appearing is to His lovers. Who are His lovers, if not those whose eyes are opened in faith and whose hearts are open and waiting for Him to show us His goodness in everything? *To trust and believe Him—this is our part.* . . . Now I will tell you what I was shown about the Giver of these gifts, for they are not more important than He.

After this, it was once again granted to me to see God—to perceive Him in a different way than I had ever seen Him before. The seeing was only for an instant. I did not envision God in a certain "form" but in my understanding, and it was this I came to know:

I saw that God is present in all things. I had to still the voice of my own mind in order to contemplate what I had seen. And after, I was given to know that *God is at work to accomplish everything that is done.*

This, revealed to my soul, caused me to be overcome with the holy grandeur of it . . . caused me to bow my soul before Him in awe and in the gentlest time of worship. . . .

For in order to take benefit from the three gifts, we must come to know that everything is done by Him, no matter how small. *Nothing occurs by chance.* Everything is working together according to God's forethought and His wise planning, which is from of old. And if a thing seems "chance" in our sight it is only because of our blindness and lack of ability to understand the vastness of the plan and greatness of God himself, who is the beginning and end of all things. . . .

And so I found myself to have received something more from the gift of faith: the endless happiness and rest that come in knowing everything that is done is *well done.*

How this is so, when fallen creatures and sin are involved, I did not know. Nor was I shown at this time how sinfulness can be made to work together for good. (I was shown at another time, as I shall later tell.) I only know for sure that the Lord does not sin. But in the light of God's presence, these questions were swept aside for the moment.

I found all I wanted was to fix His "image" before the eyes of my soul—that is, a knowledge of the high, perfect grandeur of our Lord and of all His vast works. The works that are kept secret from us at present, as well as those that are being revealed.

In this way, God was shown to my soul, and also the rightfulness of all His dealings. At least He was shown to me to the capacity this poor soul could grasp. . . .

Faith must convert you from your blind judgments about God to a true view of Him. Then—you will see how all the works it pleases the Lord to do are lovely, easy, and sweet. I promise that, once you see Him in this way, it will bring you endless joy. And it will give you power to silence the doubting voice within.

Contemplate this truth, then. Fix it like a firm foundation on which your soul may stand. It is a perfect gift from God to your soul. . . .

My Generous Father—today I ask for the gift of your wisdom and insight. Show me how everyone in my life—and every circumstance I am walking through—is a perfect gift, sent from you.

Let your presence be with me as I open every gift you give—especially the ones that are so difficult to accept.

15
He Made Us for Himself

The LORD *is exalted . . . his glory [is] above the heavens. Who is like the* LORD *our God, the One who sits enthroned on high, who stoops down to look on the heavens and the earth?*

Psalm 113:4–6

[See my servant]. . . . He was despised and rejected by men . . . and we esteemed him not . . . he was pierced for our transgressions, he was crushed for our iniquities. . . .

Isaiah 53:3, 5

In Christ, the fullness of God met the weakness of mortal flesh and all of our humanity. He who is the highest, the most worthy to receive honor from all created things—He was wickedly brought low by sinful men and hateful powers, and treated in the most foul manner.

It is the Passion of our Lord we need to grasp. Therefore, I will continue to remind you that it will do you endless good to meditate on this fact: *God willingly suffered for you, because of love.*

Once again, I was contemplating the cross of Christ. And I was given to understand why the Lord Jesus—the exalted One, the Prince of Heaven, the radiance of invisible God—descended into a created, fleshly body. For it is unfathomable that He took on the substance of man in its weakness and need, even though we are precious to God.

Now a new thought came: He had to do this in order to come into our estate—into our small kingdom where we are so misled in thinking we are safe and secure. Inside these blinding walls of flesh, we are most terrified to suffer in even the smallest way, and so our "estate" is a prison in which our spirit is condemned. And worse still, we are blind to the fact that we are in a prison! And if we cannot see our plight, how can we look for the way of escape? How can we experience the freedom of living in spirit above our flesh?

Because we are so imprisoned in our lower nature, Jesus took on tender flesh. And after doing so, He set out on His mission—which was to meet a suffering and humiliation worse than any man has ever felt or could feel. Worse, I say, because of the heights of bliss and endless glory from which He had come down. Worse, because of the honor, worship, and thanks that are due to Him.

He took on the suffering for the sin of every

man and woman who is to be saved. He saw our sorrows—*every one of our sorrows!* All our despair, all our anguish, He wrapped around himself as He bore our flesh. Nothing we can experience in the flesh was *outside* of Christ. . . .

And then the Lord formed a question in my mind: *Do you see now that my suffering took in all you can suffer, in order that you may know I alone am the One who can satisfy you in times of greatest distress and pain and need?*

When I found my voice, I answered. "Yes, Lord—what can I offer you but all my thanks? *Yes*, my good Lord—I bless you!"

Then Jesus, our most gracious Lord said, *This is very good. For you must understand it was my mission to bring your spirit within my own Spirit. Only in me, in spirit, will you find complete peace, rest, and satisfaction. Therefore, when you find your spiritual satisfaction in me, my work is complete in you. This is how my work is rewarded and I am honored.*

When I saw how Christ is honored, my understanding was lifted up to heaven. And I was given to know the pleasure the Father himself has in Jesus, His princely and obedient Son. He is well-pleased with the work of His Son, which accomplishes our salvation. For we were created to be a courteous gift of love—a gift with which the Father honors the Son. . . .

That was when the wonder of it all took me.
We are His joy. His reward. His honor.
We are His crown.

I cannot tell you the endless wonder I found in contemplating this knowledge:

We are His completion and crown. . . .

*M*y Father—heaven and earth are *contained in you!*

You say I am the crowning achievement of your creation—but I do not know how to hold this truth wisely. I slide so easily into self-glory or self-pity, depending on whether others esteem me or not.

Let me come to rest in your hands, then . . . knowing I am a gift that is fully at your disposal . . . and knowing you will never misuse me, never waste me, never forget me.

16

He Gives Us Faith

*Against all hope, Abraham in hope believed . . . he did
not waver through unbelief regarding the promise of
God, but was strengthened in his faith and gave glory
to God, being fully persuaded that God had power to do
what he had promised.*

———

Romans 4:18, 20–21

*T*hough Jesus could only suffer once in His
tender human flesh, He never ceases to offer us the
same unending goodness. Do you understand what
is promised to us in this?

On the cross, and in His death, He showed us
the depths of His love and goodness. It was a
display of His love—not just *in* that hour, *for* that
hour—but as a river that constantly pours forth
from Him by His Spirit. So His compassion flows to
us without ever ceasing.

Every day, He is ready to accomplish for you
and for me whatever is required for the salvation,

healing, comfort, nurture, and strengthening of our souls. If it were needed, if it were possible, He would even go to the cross for us again.

As Christians we marvel that, in the end of time, Jesus will come back for us and re-create the heavens and the earth. I mean this in no dishonoring way, but that mighty act is a thing He is able to do by the power of His word—and in comparison it is a little thing, when you understand that He would, *for love*, die for us all over again if that would strengthen us, or lift us closer to His side, or free our souls from sin. As I say, though His work for us was accomplished once and for all, He would die for us today, tomorrow, and the next day.

The death of His Son was the greatest offering the Father could make for my soul and yours. It was a sacrifice given to show His unending love. Yes, I had understood this.

Now the Lord said to my soul, *If you understand my love pours out to you without ceasing . . . and if you understand I would leave heaven again to die for you if necessary, ignoring the suffering . . . why is it you doubt I will do, for love of you, all that you truly need . . . and all that I am able?*

Father of promises kept, I need a special gift from you . . . the gift of an enlightened eye and a wise heart. Show me how all of my past was in your hand, shaping me and my life for your higher purposes. Breathe

72

into my heart the peace that comes from knowing you have always, only, acted in love for me.

Seal in me a more powerful faith . . . a faith that rests in you alone.

17
He Makes Us Clean

This is what the LORD says: "You were sold [and taken away] for nothing, and without money you will be redeemed."

Isaiah 52:3 (emphasis added)

Cleanse me . . . and I will be clean; wash me, and I will be whiter than snow . . . [for] the sacrifices of God are a broken spirit . . . and [a] contrite heart.

Psalm 51:7, 17

After I understood Christ's amazing love for us, I thought about the many years I longed to follow Him more perfectly . . . but was prevented by my own blindness and sin. Nothing had hindered me except this fallen state in which we all live. For I had long been willing, but my mind was still darkened to the unspeakable love of God in Christ for me.

In the past, many questions troubled me—but one particular question disturbed me most. If there had never been sin, then we would have remained pure, just as the Lord created us. Since God is wise and sovereign, and He knows all things that will happen before they occur—why, then, did He not prevent sin? Why did He allow us to be led down this miserable path away from His presence and into the darkness of this world? If He had intervened in any way, nothing evil would befall us, and all would have been well.

I must warn you, it is unprofitable to dwell on this question if you have not come into the light of true wisdom that is revealed in Christ. The fleshly mind wants to reason out an answer to this profound question. But an answer cannot be found if you begin with human reason and try to understand God and His ways from our lower viewpoint. There is grave danger, on this lower path, to the mind that has not first been humbled under the hand of God in the Spirit of Christ.

For myself—though I knew I should not trouble the peace of my soul by fretting over such questions—it seemed I could not help doing so. I did not see that I was beginning my search for an answer within my own human mind and from my own lower view of things. That is to say, I did not see that this is the root of pride. So I was often disturbed. And at the edges of my thoughts, I could almost hear the subtle voice questioning: *God could have stopped man from sinning. But He did not. Then how*

are we at fault? And how can God begin to judge us,
when. . . ?

You can see how foolish I was, thinking God
must explain and justify himself *before* I could trust
Him.

Nonetheless, Jesus chose to show me how His
love is poured out every day to satisfy everything
that is needful to me, as I told you before. And now
in His noble courtesy, He granted me an answer to
this question:

Sin is necessary—but all is well, and all will be well,
and all manner of things will be well.

Then He laid open to me His view of sin,
removing from my sight the outer trappings of
sin—that is, all the evil acts men do out of their evil
intention. He stripped sin to its core, as it were.
And I saw the substance of sin for what it is. . . .

Nothing at all.

Yes, beneath the outward shell—beneath the
lovely promises that temptation holds out to us—
sin is hollow. Emptiness, and nothing more. I saw
sin as the Lord sees it—including every action and
every word which does not proceed from the Lord.
When all was stripped from sin's outward
appearance—all greed and lust, all lying, stealing,
murder, meanness, hurting, and grief—the core of
sin had no substance at all. There is nothing in sin
to nourish our soul, nothing to feed us the inner life
we crave. This is why sin can never satisfy the
hunger of our soul. In fact, when we sin, our soul is
left emptier and hungrier than before.

Though sin is nothing at all, yet it can be recognized by its outer husk—that is, by the pain and grief it brings.

And then I understood, in part, the puzzling thing the Lord had said to me: *Sin is necessary. . . .* For as we follow Him who is our Master it seems He must purge and cleanse our flesh, which continues in this fallen state. Sin is what reveals to us all our inward affections—all our hungers for the corrupt spiritual food which tantalizes us. We sin, and then we experience its emptiness and pain. As our soul starves, we cry out to the Lord for help and mercy. So we are brought to Him for salvation, healing, safety . . . and all that He means to give us for the life of our soul. . . .

At last, I say, His meaning became clear to me: Our Lord, who is ever and only good, has nothing but tender love for all who are willing to come to Him and be saved. This is why He wants us to rush to Him for comfort, no matter what our sin has been. For once we are leaning close to Him— hidden with Christ in God—we can hear Him say, *It is true that sin has caused your pain and sadness . . . but now all is well, and all will be well, and all manner of things will be well.*

When I saw sin in this manner, and when I heard His words spoken with such compassion, I saw that He held no blame toward me—nor toward anyone else who will come to Him to be saved. *There was no blame!*

At last I saw how unkind and foolish it would

be of me to blame God on account of my sins, since He does not blame me but offers free and endless salvation . . . and comfort within His own arms. . . .

So I understood that God can use even sin to turn us to himself. And in that sense, sin is necessary. It can prevent the spiritual damage that would come to a soul if its greatest impurity—evil pride and haughtiness—were never challenged. It is necessary to expose the vanity of this wretched life in order to make us hunger for life eternal.

And I understood Him to say, *Yes, child, I will destroy your affections and the secret pride that binds you. Then am I able to gather your scattered soul—gather you together in my arms. Then you will be purified from the world, and set apart, through the union of your spirit with my Spirit.*

Holy and Pure Father, you have entered the gates of hell to pay for my sin. . . . You destroyed the iron manacles of shame and guilt that would hold me there.

And now I am dressed in the purity of Christ, by the gift of faith—a gift that you gave me, too! I trust you, Father, to show me my own heart . . . to cleanse the remaining corruption of self-sufficiency . . . which keeps me from loving and serving you.

18

He Is Full of Wonders

Then I saw a new heaven and a new earth, for the first heaven and the first earth had passed away. . . . He who was seated on the throne said, "I am making everything new!" Then he said, "Write this down, for these words are trustworthy and true."

Revelation 21:1, 5

For some time, I contemplated what the Lord had shown me about sin.

I found great peace in knowing that the Lord can use even sin and its grief to drive us back to himself—peace in knowing that He happily receives me into His presence, where He can show me the pride and wrong affections that cause me to sin in the first place. It gave me peace to know that, as He works the mighty power of salvation into my soul, God does all things well. And so all *will* be well.

And still, I felt a certain sense of darkness and

mourning. For I felt troubled about all the grief evil men cause the human race because of their wickedness. If God knew beforehand how innocents would suffer. . . ?

So I asked, with a great reverent fear, "Lord, I know you are only good. But I do not understand how *all things are well*, when so much harm and anguish come through sin to your dear creatures?"

I must tell you I was amazed at the meek and most loving manner in which He addressed me. I sensed in Him a tender respect toward me, the way you would feel toward an adored child who, in all innocence, has asked an embarrassing question.

First, He showed me the enormity of Adam's sin. For Adam reached out to grasp hidden knowledge that was beyond his wisdom and power to hold within his created being. Adam was like a child, stealing the weapon of his father who is a great warrior, and taking it out to his playmates—and not one of them knows the utter and irreversible devastation such a weapon will cause in their hands. Poor Adam. His was the greatest crime because, in him, was our whole race damaged.

And then the Lord showed me that Christ's atonement was far greater in its power to heal and restore than Adam's sin was harmful. By showing me this, I understood Him to say, *Since I have set right the greatest crime—a sin against the whole race—I want you to know that, through the power of my saving* hand, *I will set right every wrong which, by comparison, is less. . . .*

This part of His answer I am sure you can understand. It has given me great peace to know His salvation is a power that is even now at work in the world—like an unstoppable force.

But why was sin allowed . . . and how will He make right all the suffering sin has caused?

There *is* another answer to this, and before I tell you what He showed me, I must speak to you about the secrets of God. The Lord gave me to know that some things are hidden and closed to us for now, kept within the secret counsels of God. Just as it is right for a governor or king to keep certain strategies, reasons, and plans secret before their time, so it is right for God to do the same. Surely you can see this. And it is not fitting or wise for the servants to pry or demand to know these secret plans.

The Lord is not angry at those who press about such questions—"Why do the innocent suffer? Why does God continue to allow sin?" More, He feels pity and compassion on us when we destroy our own peace of mind—for the answer is so great, and our minds are not ready to receive it.

The Lord wants us to leave our souls in peace, and to please Him, by leaving these profound questions alone for now. We should take as our example the saints who have gone before us, and who stand before Him now. They want to know nothing but what God chooses to show them. Their love and will is entirely folded into His. We would do immeasurable good to ourselves to practice this kind of blessed rest in God! . . .

I began to sense that the Lord has a powerful work, which is to come. For I understood Him to say, *Do not be troubled. You will see for yourself that all manner of things will be well. For now, accept this in faith. Trust in me. In the end you will see, and your amazement will be boundless.*

And now I will tell you what I was shown.

There is a single marvelous act which the whole Godhead, the blessed Trinity, is waiting and longing to perform at the last day. What this action will be, and how it will be performed is hidden from every creature who is inferior to Christ our Lord. And it must remain secret until it is performed. God, in His goodness and wisdom, wants us to know His marvelous act will be accomplished. And in His goodness and wisdom, He wants us to understand it is in our best interest for Him to conceal the act from us for now.

This marvelous act was ordained by our Lord from all eternity. It is treasured and concealed in His heart, known only to himself. I am telling you there is a high mystery, hidden in God—a marvelous act so full of wonders He cannot begin to reveal it to us now. By this one marvelous act, He makes all things well. Just as God was so powerful He made everything from nothing, in the same way He will make everything well that is not well. . . .

Knowing our good and holy God contains this

secret in himself made my soul leap with a strange longing I cannot explain. I felt like a child leaping up to try to seize a gift its father is holding in his hands. And I know that when He opens to us the full truth, we shall all marvel and rejoice in Him forever.

My Trustworthy and True Father, you who walk the deepest passages of my soul, is this the secret sin that allows all other sin to enter—my unwillingness to trust you completely when I cannot see or understand?

I come to stand before you, loving Father. Do your deep work in me. . . .

Kill my pride. Lead me out of my self into you.

19
He Gives Us His Power

[Jesus told the crowd, gathered before him near the Sea of Galilee,] "The kingdom of heaven is like a mustard seed, which a man took and planted in his field. Though it is the smallest of all your seeds, yet when it grows, it is the largest of garden plants and becomes a tree. . . ."

Matthew 13:31–32

Jesus told [Thomas], "Because you have seen me, you have believed; blessed are those who have not seen and yet have believed."

John 20:29

I had been troubling about the matter of miracles—the fact that some pray and are delivered from their bodily sufferings, and some are not.

The Lord gave to my understanding these simple thoughts on the matter: *It is well-known that I* have performed miracles in times past. It is true that my works are bountiful, full of wonders and splendor. They display the radiance of my eternal glory, penetrating into your dark, fallen, and broken world.

The first thing I knew He was instructing me about miracles was this: *What I have done in the past, I always go on doing—today and tomorrow, just as before. And I will continue to perform miraculous acts for all time to come.*

He has not changed—He will not change!

I was also given to know, *Before I perform a miracle, there must come turmoil and pain. There must come trial.*

By this I understood our trials reveal to us our soul's deepest weaknesses—all the things on which we set our security, all that we allow to take the place of the Lord. These must be revealed to us so we can see them for the powerless things they are and turn instead to the Lord. For only when we see our soul's weakness and disease are we ready to cry to the Lord and receive His help and empowering grace.

Third, He showed me, *Miracles will always come after great suffering.*

And I was given to know, some miracles will be for the outer man, to display the great power of Him who created our flesh. And some miracles will be to the benefit of our inner man—for it is in the inner man the kingdom of heaven is growing, small and at first invisible to the eye, like the outbursting of a seed within the ground. And these inward miracles come to reveal the power of heaven to sustain weak mortal flesh, to display to the world the joy of heaven that lifts our soul above the pains of the body—that is, as much as heaven can be revealed in this life, which is but a passing fog.

All of this was shown me to strengthen and increase my faith and yours, and to increase our hope in the love of God for us.

Therefore, it pleases God that we worship Him as the God who performs miracles today. For He does not want us to be heavy-spirited and depressed by the troubles, small and great, that will come to each of us. No, not at all.

For trials must always come before God can reveal himself to us, in us, and through us to the world.

My Father, one of the greatest miracles is your ability to bring to life a dead soul, to open dried eyes with the vision of faith. . . .

Let the small seed of your life inside me grow . . . until you can use me in spiritual power to perform your mighty acts.

20

He Makes Us Grow

Be completely humble and gentle; be patient, bearing with one another in love . . . until we all reach unity in the faith and in the knowledge of the Son of God and become mature. . . .

Ephesians 4:2, 13

God brought to my mind an urgent matter. I sensed He wanted to show me something more about the sin that causes us all to stumble. But at first, I was so caught up in the beauty of the Lord— wrapped up in the *good feelings* that came to me in worshiping Him—that I was paying no attention to *Him!*

In His mercy, He waited for me to move beyond my own fleshly senses. In fact, He issued a grace that stirred me from the sleep of flesh and awakened me to be attentive to Him in spirit.

The Lord gave me to understand I would experience failure and sin. I thought He wanted to show me something about my own particular failings—and that is so characteristic of our self-centeredness. Immediately, I felt anxious—anxiety and reverent fear. Can you imagine—standing in the presence of Him who is holy and seeing your future sins revealed before you?

But in the same moment, I was given to understand His mind in revealing this to me, as if He were saying to all of us: *I want to show you that I protect you, even while you are in the midst of your failing and sin.* He awakened me to see something that is generally for all Christians . . . and it is for you.

I cannot describe to you the strong sense of love and assurance given to me when words came. . . . This has made me love my brothers and sisters in Christ more than anything else. (For nothing causes irritation and anger among us except our sins and failings toward one another.)

For God allowed me to sense His love for every one of us who is being saved—love in exactly the same measure, as if we were but one soul, and not many. More than this, I understood that in every soul who will be saved God has planted His Spirit, and so the soul possesses a new godly will that does not want to sin and never agrees to sin. And yet there is a lower will, belonging to our fallen nature, which cannot desire to do anything that is not low and self-centered.

God sees these two natures constantly—and even when we forget, they are at war in us. And it is *because* we are like children, struggling to walk on

88

broken legs, that He is moved in great compassion toward us, and He eternally delights in us and rushes to aid us in our struggle.

By this, the Lord showed me how completely He loves us. We stand in His sight, and He loves us now just as much as the day when we will pass from this life into heaven to be transformed into His likeness when we behold His face.

It is love, then, that He showed me. The fire of His love that draws us all to Him. Love that purges and cleanses and refines us from our sin. Love that will complete us.

And all our sin toward one another results from this: The lower creature does not know how much it is loved by God, and so we live in darkness and selfish fear, afraid to give and forgive.

So love must fill us and replace our emptiness and sin, for all our turmoil and hardness toward each other result from lack of love.

My Father, I am always seeking assurances . . . that I am loved . . . that I am not overlooked . . . and that I am forgiven.

Thank you that you have settled these issues. Now my self-centered anxieties can lose their hold as I go on to mature in you . . . to assure others . . . to love . . . to esteem . . . to forgive.

21
He Speaks Within Us

This is what the LORD Almighty says: ". . . I am coming, and I will live among you . . . in that day [you] will become my people. . . . Be still before the LORD . . . because he has roused himself from his holy dwelling."

Zechariah 2:8, 10–11, 13

[Jesus] was transfigured before them. His face shone like the sun, and his clothes became as white as the light . . . a bright cloud enveloped them, and a voice from the cloud said, "This is my Son, whom I love; with him I am well pleased. Listen to him!"

Matthew 17:2, 5 (emphasis added)

What is it that unites the soul within us—the lower part which does not want to do God's will, with the new man who longs to do the Father's will without failure?

It is *prayer*. I mean the kind of prayer that unites us to God. The kind of prayer that does not merely ask for things and answers, after which we walk away from God and go about our earthly business.

Many Christians do not understand the kind of prayer I am talking about, in which the voice of the lower nature is stilled and our spirit is caused to wait like a beloved servant before its Master. For it is in this blessed stillness He may speak to us living words of life and healing and freedom.

Many believe it is enough that their souls have been restored to God and are like God in nature and substance because they have received His saving grace. Yet they may wonder why they are not like Him in actual condition—and that is because sin is still having its way. They may wonder why they cannot cause God to do what they ask.

The kind of prayer I am talking about, as I have said, is the kind in which we wait silently before the Lord. We allow Him to show us everything within that is set against His will. We rarely pray in this way because we fear what He may do to us if we abandon ourselves to His will.

You will know that you have experienced true prayer when your soul witnesses within you that you will as He wills—that your wills are one. Only this kind of prayer frees the conscience from the condemning voices within us. Only this kind of prayer prepares the soul to receive God's strengthening grace—strength, I say, both to overcome sin and to perform the will of the Father.

This is what our Lord Jesus meant when He told us to pray and believe that we have what we ask. (See Matthew 21:22.) He teaches us to pray in order to bring our will in line with the Father's will, and to firmly trust He will accomplish the work He shows us to do. For He looks upon us in love, and wants to restore us as partners—rebels that we are—in His endless good workings. . . .

This is the beginning of the soul's true prayer: We wait upon the Lord and allow Him to show himself to our soul. For when we behold His presence within us, we have everything our soul longs for. In that moment, we feel there is nothing more we could ask for, and all our powers are focused on contemplating Him. . . . For the first reason we pray is to have the straying, scattered affections of our soul drawn together into the vision of Him as He is.

This makes possible the second part of prayer. When our spirit is settled in a wonderful reverence for Him—feeling so much sweetness and delight in Him alone that we care for nothing but His will—it is then His Spirit will move in us. So the thing we pray is exactly what He moves us to pray at that time. (See Romans 8.) . . .

You may say your soul is too often tempted, troubled, and restless to pray. I tell you, that is exactly when you should pray as I have just told you—for the prayer of silence and waiting is the way to take hold of your unruly soul and keep it still until it is lovingly focused on God, made supple, and ready to move again at His word of loving direction.

And you may as well know this, too. By no kind of prayer do we make God bend to us.

Father of the Living Word, I know you hear every word, even before I pray to you.

Now I will be still, and wait for you to speak your word in me . . . the word that shows you are alive and active in this world through me.

22
He Is Higher

The LORD said to me, ". . . Do not be afraid of [anyone], for I am with you and will rescue you."

Jeremiah 1:7–8

In God, whose word I praise, in God I trust; I will not be afraid. What can mortal man do to me?

Psalm 56:4

God does not judge as men judge, and that is a very good thing.

Men look on the superficial aspects of our being, on all that is changeable—based on looks and our emotional state. One day we seem one way, and the next day we seem another, and it is rare that anything but the least part of our true hidden nature is fully expressed in our outward manner.

So the judgment of men—all but the most spiritually wise—is mixed with their own faulty and incomplete perceptions of us. I am sure you have found that some people dislike you for what

94

seems no reason at all, and their opinion of you is harsh and unwarranted. At the same time others accept you and like you no matter what you do— and from a godly perspective they are not doing your soul very much good by indulging you and being too lenient.

Even so, the judgment of men *can* be used by God to help us, if our souls are open to receive from Him at all times and in all things. When people speak kind words of correction and good judgment, we should receive them as from the Lord. And when they speak harshly, painfully, we can pass their words through His grace and mercy—asking Him to show us the kernel of truth that lies beneath the bitter or accusing tone. Because Jesus suffered to bring us into God's kingdom, every judgment can be turned to our good—that is, it can steer us in the course God has for us.

For people and their words do not govern our souls, whether those words are kind and flattering, or condemning. But we are governed in spirit by the loving justice of God, who purchased our souls—if we but recognize that all things are available to His use, and if we will recognize Him in all things.

My Father, show me those people whose good opinion I crave, and whose disapproval I fear.

I will stop allowing my life to be governed by the will and disposition and words of others . . . so I may be free to live and move with respect only for your governing will. For I know you are higher than any other.

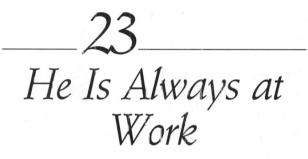

23

He Is Always at Work

I trust in your unfailing love. . . . I will sing to the LORD for he has been good to me.

Psalm 13:5–6

Redeem us because of your unfailing love.

Psalm 44:26

---

*I*n just a little while, we will see our Lord clearly. We will see *in Him* all that we desire. Then we will marvel that we could have hungered, and demanded, and sinned in this life. For it is our blindness and hunger that cause us to strive for things that are so much less than He—things so little as to be nothing. And yet we do hunger for these things, and we do turn away from Him. It seems we are so uneven in our spiritual growth, sometimes growing in the character of Christ . . .

and sometimes behaving like perfect children of the devil!

That is why—though the Lord had shown me He is not angry with us—I wondered about the unceasing love of God, which I had been shown. For I had been taught that we must see our sin and turn from it, and *then* God's anger is turned away, then we are forgiven and experience His mercy. . . .

But in the Lord's revelation of His love to me, I had not detected *any* holding back of love. It seemed impossible that God, who is love, could withhold any part of love for us until *after* we turn to Him. I saw only love.

So I sought Him in contemplation. And now I shall describe as best I can how God's mercy operates, if God will give me the grace to do so.

In this life, we are so unstable—even the best Christian among us. We say we love God one minute, and truly do love Him. And in the next minute we fall into sin—one minute speaking well of people, then slandering them behind their backs, or freely overlooking the sins of those we favor and refusing to forgive those we do not think "worthy" of forgiveness. We fall into these sins because we are blind to ourselves, ignorant of the great evil we are doing. We are weak and foolish in our self-centeredness. Add to that all the sickness and sad events of life that overpower our good intentions. . . .

Chief among our problems is that we are blind to God. For if we could live with Him in view at all times, knowing His benevolence in everything, then we would have no reason to hold hard feelings toward anyone. We would be free of the fear and spiritual hunger that cause us to sin. . . .

So it is that, in His dealings with us, God must begin and end with *mercy*. . . . For we cannot live with perpetual spiritual revelation of Him in this life; there is so much to distract us and destroy our peace. And the moment our spiritual eyes turn from Him to attend to the business of this world, we are prone to forget what we saw in Him. And almost at once we are pitched into sin.

Before we know it, we are not conscious of God's mercy but of the sin that is in us. Do you see it? I am referring to our old enemy, the root of pride. For in our pride we elevate our own sin above the power of God, above the vision of who He really is. . . .

That is why our good Lord, the Holy Spirit who is endless life, dwells within our soul. He protects us as we stumble around, blindly forgetful of the love of God. He produces in us a longing for peace, a longing for freedom from restlessness. By His working within us, which we call grace, He brings us to rest. He works in us, and He does so to reveal our own dissatisfaction to us. Once we see we are dissatisfied we are then willing to turn and become obedient under the hand of God.

We do not reconcile ourselves to God, then. *It is God who works in us, drawing us to himself, reconciling us, giving us the will to obey.* Do you see any anger in this? Do you see God withholding forgiveness and mercy until after we have turned back to Him? To say so is blindness and spiritual pride.

For this is the way God leads us all throughout this life, in which we are so unsteady in ourselves. This is how God operates in the soul, in His mercy. . . .

I saw no anger or unforgiveness in God. I only saw these faults in us. And our anger is a perversity, for it is we who refuse to forgive, thinking the sins of others are greater than our own. So we set our own souls in opposition to peace and love.

Father of Unfailing Love, I declare today a day of rest, happiness, and celebration throughout my soul.

For you have redeemed *me . . . and you are* freeing *me . . . and you will* never leave *me—not even for a moment. I ask that you continue your good work in me until all that's in me is in obedience to your law of love.*

24

He Removes the Root

The LORD has laid on [his Servant] the iniquity of us all . . . it was the LORD's will to crush him and cause him to suffer . . . and after the suffering of his soul, he will see the light of life and be satisfied. . . .

Isaiah 53:5, 10–11

*I*n the wondrous "showing" I told you about earlier—involving the lord and his manservant—I saw this also. . . .

The lord spoke secretly to the servant, sending him out to a certain place to do a certain task. Then the servant hastened as fast as he could run, loving to do the lord's will. . . .

. . . only to fall into a wooded valley, where he was greatly injured. There he lay, greatly confused and moaning in extreme pain. Writhing, he was unable to raise himself. His clothes were torn to shreds by cruel thorns. He was left there all alone, helpless. And the worst pain was that he could no longer see his master's face. It was this that caused

him finally to cry out in utter wretchedness of spirit. . . .

I wondered at the servant's falling, for there is no fault in Christ. I looked to the eyes of the master. . . .

In the lord's eyes were only love and compassion and pleasure in his manservant. For the servant had set out only to do his master's will. And even in his extreme pain the servant's will remained intent on completing the task he was sent to do.

The fall, then, was the descent of Christ into the valley of the womb, within a maiden who was the fairest daughter of Adam.

And I saw how the clothing was torn . . . for the clothing was His flesh. For evil men spared Him no pain, and his skin was torn with rods and scourges, thorns and nails, pulling apart His tender flesh, which dried and stuck to the bones while He was yet living.

When I saw Him writhing, this was revealed to me:

He could never rise from this fleshly estate—not even with all his mighty power—from the time He descended into the maiden's womb until his body was slain and dead. For He had completely given over His soul into the Father's hands, with all mankind for whom He was sent. . . .

And when the servant had suffered greatly and was dead—then did he begin to show his true strength. For I saw him go down into hell. And there he seized a great hideous twisted mass, like a dark root, and tore it out of the depths.

And the dark thing I saw was the soul of man, which was rightly made not for hell but to be joined with Christ in heaven.

Then I understood, as never before, why it was the Father's will to permit His Son—both in nature and in fleshly form—to suffer every one of our pains. Not to spare Him at all for our sake . . . not even in the least.

My Rescuing Father, because Jesus, your own Son, was crushed for me, to fulfill your will . . . give me the same courage and power.

Today, give me your strength to face the low and foolish and evil desires that root my soul in sins and keep me from walking free and whole in you.

25
He Tends Our Soul

[Jesus] told them many things in parables, saying: "A farmer went out to sow his seed . . . some fell along the path . . . some fell on rocky places . . . other seed fell among thorns . . . still other seed fell on good soil, where it produced a crop. . . . He who has ears, let him hear."

Matthew 13:3–5, 7–9

[Jesus said,] "Even now the [gardener] draws his wages, even now he harvests the crop for eternal life."

John 4:36

Sometime later, I was again shown the same wondrous scene I have described to you—of the lord, with his manservant standing before him. At least it was very nearly the same. For now I saw something else beyond the servant's fall and his suffering. . . .

I saw there was a treasure on the earth, which the lord loved very much, and this was the cause of the manservant's going out.

I was greatly surprised, because this lord was so high and great I could not imagine what there could be upon the lowly earth he would desire at all. But it seemed this treasure would satisfy some deep longing or hunger, and so I supposed it was some sort of rare food for which he yearned.

This time when the lord sent out his manservant, I watched carefully, wondering what manner of work the servant was going to do. And I understood he was being sent to do the hardest work there is. . . .

The servant was sent out to be the gardener of a far-distant garden that was dearly beloved to his lord. In this garden there grows a food, as it were, that is pleasing to the lord.

And so the servant began to labor and sweat. He dug beneath the hot sun, digging deep ditches—both to till the soil deeply and make it ready for good seed, and to create ditches to catch the waters from heaven so they might flow throughout the whole garden . . . ditches prepared to receive the waters of heaven when they fall in their due season.

His work was to make ready the garden of his lord, planting fine seed and getting it ready for the sweet waters to flow. In this way, the garden would produce the very best fruit, and plenty of it! And the servant was not to cease his labor until he had prepared all the food of the garden that would be pleasing to his lord. . . .

My Patient Father, Sower of Eternal Life, till and tend my heart. In every temptation, and in every opposition—open me more deeply so the seed of your Word will penetrate deeper to the core of my being.

Pour the life of your Spirit like water through me. Let your truth be proven in the fruit of my life . . . in everything I say and do . . . for your enjoyment, and to your honor.

26

He Never Condemns

There is now no condemnation for those who are in Christ Jesus. . . . Those who live in accordance with the Spirit have their minds set on what the Spirit desires. . . . The Spirit himself testifies with our spirit that we are God's children.

Romans 8:1, 5, 16

Our Lord, who is our gardener, knows this about us:

In our lifetime, we are a marvelous mixture both of well-being and also many troubles.

That is, we carry in us our Lord Jesus and all the spiritual blessings that are ours in Him because of His rising. (See Ephesians 1:3.) And we also carry in us the blindness, misery, and wretched harm caused to us by Adam's falling.

And so we are dying and constantly protected by Christ. He touches us with His graces, and little by little we are raised to greater trust in Him and His salvation.

And we are blind—foolishly forgetting to trust Him so often, almost the moment we turn our eyes away from Him to our outward circumstances. For in our fallen state, the senses of our flesh and the affections of our soul are so affected by feelings and sins. And it is this flesh that makes us so blind and darkened in spirit. So much so that we can scarcely accept the comforting of our Lord, though He dwells right within us and eagerly offers His strength with open hands.

Because of this double-mindedness—this gray half-light of spirit in which we miserably dwell most of the time—it is important we take this action on our own behalf: *Make it your intention to wait patiently for God to show himself faithful, merciful, gracious, and good, whether the circumstances you are in are good or evil to your lower understanding. Trust Him to pour out mercy and the strength of grace.*

Beyond our own choosing, though, there is the matter of His working. For it is God who is at work in us, to open the eye of our understanding by which we have spiritual sight—more at times, and less at other times. And all of this is according to the ability God himself gives us.

And so at times we are allowed to rise with the mind of Christ. And at times we stumble into our fleshly blindness. . . .

It is true we will remain in this mixed mind all the days of our life. And that is why the Lord

wants us to cultivate a deep and abiding trust—
until we know of a certainty that He is with us
always, in every circumstance. (See Matthew 28:20.)

And if we fall through our own blind and
foolish devices, let us not remain in our fallen
condition, thinking He has despised and forsaken
us. Let us quickly get up again, remembering He
does not fault us and will not even scold us. (See
Colossians 1:21–23.)

Rise quickly from your stumbling, in the
strength of Christ, as soon as you are aware of your
wretched sin. Willingly make amendments in your
inner self, paying attention to root out the attitude
within—that secret inclination, which was revealed
in the outward action of your sin. So you cooperate
with the work of your soul's gardener.

After that I say, rise quickly and go on your
way in the love of God.

M*y Father, if you do not condemn me,
then why do I belittle and condemn myself?*

*If you do not look with anger or disgust at my
failings—but you offer compassion and help—why do I
hesitate to come to you sooner?*

27

He Seals Our Heart

The Lord said, ". . . [My chosen one] will chase after her lovers but not catch them. . . . Then she will say, 'I will go back to my husband as at first, for then I was better off than now.' . . . Therefore I am now going to allure her; I will lead her into the desert and speak tenderly to her. . . . There she will sing as in the days of her youth. . . ."

Hosea 1:9; 2:7, 14–15

Our Lord wishes for us to know another important truth, about the mixed nature that is in us, and about our walk "in Christ."

Many Christians are well aware that the weak lower nature remains in them even after they come to Christ—the nature that causes us to look away from Him and, inevitably, stumble and fall. This causes them so much discouragement, for they do not like the feeling of failure that comes, and many give up their walk along the spiritual way.

"What's the good of trying to be so 'spiritual' and high-minded?" they say. "If I am only going to fail, and feel so terrible afterward—why put myself through so much grief, trying hard to be a spiritual person?" Such questions are asked by the mind in its lower estate.

I have told you, it is the Lord's will that we walk by the light of our faith and not by our human sight or understanding. (See 2 Corinthians 5:7.) For the Lord's whole blessed will is *for* us—all of His goodness and strength are kept for us in Christ Jesus. And in the eyes of God it is as if we are already betrothed to our Bridegroom, and united with Him in "one flesh," as it were. It is God's intention that our soul never be parted from His Son Christ—for our return and union with His Son was in His mind and heart from of old. . . .

This is what you must know and fix in your heart—that God never *began* to love mankind at some particular moment. For just as we know we will be with Him for endless ages to come, He has loved us from ages past without beginning. For His love has no beginning and no end. And so, in His intentions for us, we were never parted from His Son—though we were blind and lost to His intention.

Here is the marvel: Even before He made us, knowing our failing that was to come, *He loved us.* And when we were first made in Adam we loved Him at first sight. And so our union was sealed by a spiritual substance, a force that proceeded into

111

our soul from the Holy Spirit to make us know whose we are and to whom we belong. (See Ephesians 1:13.)

What is the substance of this seal? It is nothing other than love. If we were not given the ability, we would not be able to know love, or to desire it, or to give it in return. And so love is the wedding gift of the Holy Spirit, given to us in the Son to prepare us for the coming wedding feast. (See 1 Corinthians 13:13.)

For love, then, let us always rise and continue on in Christ, moving closer to the day of our final wondrous union. . . . In endless love we are led on, surrounded and protected by God, and we will never be lost.

My Powerful Father, I am amazed when I stop to consider this: You have always loved me—you have never stopped loving me.

Today . . . in this moment . . . I rise from my failings . . . I turn from the deceptive voices, whose promises are impotent and empty.

In spirit, I come to be surrounded and protected by your might. And sealed with the mark of your Spirit . . . a pure love for you.

28

He Lives in Us

Be strong in the Lord and in his mighty power.

Ephesians 6:10

*[The glorious Father offers] incomparably great power
for us who believe. That power is like the working of his
mighty strength, which he exerted in Christ when he
raised him from the dead and seated him at his right
hand in the heavenly realms. . . .*

Ephesians 1:19–20

Since we are united to Christ in spirit, God
makes no distinction between our blessed Lord
Jesus and the least soul that is to be saved. For the
love of God is not measured out in "degrees." His
love is endless.

. . . We are one with Christ.

But do we understand this, in even the smallest
part? We must grasp what this means, for it is the
foundation of true faith. . . .

For we are enclosed in the Father, enclosed in

the Son, and enclosed in the Holy Spirit. And incredible as this seems, the Father, the Son, and the Holy Spirit are enclosed in us—our God, who is almighty, all wise, all goodness. . . .

It is this experience of the life of God within us that is the ground and bedrock of our true faith—not our doctrine and teaching only. For we are called to a living faith. It is the living Spirit that stirs and awakens our soul and makes us experience a longing for God. It is the Spirit that brings the force of God's eternal life into us. For His power contains all strength, all health, and all spiritual vitality.

Without this living faith, then, it is impossible for us to receive any strength or might from the Lord. For faith comes when we experience our relationship to the Lord, when we see with our heart how He lives His life in and through us. This is the basis of all our belief. This is what gives us strength and certainty—when we come to trust God with our whole being.

Nothing is more wonderfully assuring than to have this knowledge: *We are in God, treasured, cared for, and protected. And He is in us, growing in us the powerful fruits of His life, which is without end.* . . .

Draw your life from God in Christ. This is what makes us grow as children of God. This is what gives strength to your soul as you live in this dark and challenging world.

Father of All Might, you have planted in me, by your Spirit, fertile seeds of eternal life and strength.

I surrender all of myself to you—heart, mind, and muscle. Show me, today, what that means as I move among a world of people whom you also love.

He Searches Our Heart

The lamp of the LORD searches the spirit of a man; it searches out his inmost being.

Proverbs 20:27

On another day, I was again contemplating what I had been shown about the mixture of affections that troubles our soul in this life.

I saw that it is surely easier and quicker for us to come to a knowledge of God than it is to know our own murky soul, disturbed as it is by rampant affections.

But in the innermost place of our soul, there is God. He is the Creator and foundation of our soul. We are so firmly grounded in God—and so highly treasured by Him—that it is wiser to fix our soul in the knowledge of God first. And then, by comparison with His wisdom and loving intent for us, we can come to know our soul aright.

In the light of God's being we can rightly

discern our own motives and correct them.

For is He not our soul's Creator, and the source of our true life? He is . . . and He is also the power that holds the very essence of our spirit within the gross flesh we inhabit. (See Colossians 1:16–17.) Realize, then, that you are only complete in Christ—for it is growing in the nature and character of Christ that brings your fallen, stubborn flesh into obedient submission to your spirit. (See Romans 7– 8:1.) Christ is the One who draws together your scattered and restless soul into one purpose.

This, then, is the soul's first task, the one "labor" in spirit that will heal, feed, strengthen: *Fix the eyes of your inward man on God, until you understand that your only life is in God.*

God is your soul's home and its only safe dwelling. So, as I say, see with the eyes of your soul that *in God* you stand firm and unshakable. In this way you will also come to know your own soul. Dwell on the character of God so that you know Him in whom we are fully enclosed—and you will gain strength in the Spirit to escape the half-light of self-deception. As you contemplate the invisible beauty and goodness of God, the spiritual light that radiates from His character will pass within you. His light will shine upon all that is concealed in darkness within you.

Let His light reveal to you the true nature of your heart's motives and plans—all that you want to call "innocent" when, in fact, it is false and dangerous . . . and deadly to your soul.

As we learn to walk free of our darkness—by the power of His Spirit—we will come to know ourselves as we were created to be—that is, the children of God.

So I insist, it is only in God we can know our own heart. Only in Him can we find our true risen nature, which has been lost to us.

My Father—Living Light! Your light approaches . . . and I feel the stirring of shame. I thank you that your Spirit walks with me into the darkness inside to show me what is really crouching there . . . my wounded self-love, which hates to be exposed.

Today let me leave behind the wounded, hiding creature . . . knowing that as I walk with you in the light I will heal . . . and grow strong.

30

He Pours Out Grace

*T*his is what the Lord says: "I will extend peace to
[you] like a river. . . . As a mother comforts her child, so
will I comfort you; and you will be comforted. . . . When
you see this, your heart will rejoice. . . ."

Isaiah 66:12–14

*G*race and peace [come] to you from God our Father
and the Lord Jesus Christ . . . for through [the grace
that is ours in] Christ our comfort overflows.

2 Corinthians 1:2, 5 (editor's notes added)

*I*n Christ, and by His might, the dark root of sin
is torn out. In Him, by Him, we are lifted out of
hell—and also set free from all the misery of this
earthly life.

. . . And our walk in the life of salvation must
be continued by grace. For grace is nothing other

119

than the strength of the Holy Spirit, penetrating deeper and deeper into every dark place within our soul, where the light of Christ must be shed to call us further out of darkness. (See 1 Peter 1:9.)

By the working of grace, every dark place within us *will* be penetrated—length and breadth, height and depth. For our complete freedom is the will of our loving Father.

I must tell you how this grace operates. And I want to say why it is necessary for God, by His Holy Spirit, to penetrate the thick walls with which we, in our self-centered pride, have surrounded our soul—until we keep our true self hidden from everyone including God . . . or so we think.

The Lord seemed to show me that He begins to work in us by a love more tender and sweet than that of a mother. Is it not the love of God that bids us come out of hiding and return to our natural place within His kindness and unfailing care? Is it not the Word of Truth, the living seed, that penetrates our selfish darkness? Yes, to come into Christ is, in a way, coming back into the womb of love in which we were created. And when we are born of the Spirit and come into our right minds, we realize we are the children of God. Then we know that the One who is tenderness and love has never left us to ourselves—though we have left Him. . . .

Now our human mothers bear us into a lower life of pain and death. Though we cling to this world with all our might—what is it that we hold

120

to so tightly? A vapor. But Jesus, with eternal love, stronger than any human mother's, has birthed us into endless life. *Praise to Him, and all blessings!* . . .

A human mother nourishes her newborn with the sweet milk of her own breast. Jesus feeds us with himself. First, He nourishes our soul with the milk of His Word . . . by which He makes us strong and leads us, right at His side, every step of the way. In Him we grow up and gain more understanding of the Father, and of the grace and joy that pour into us from heaven itself. Then we are strong enough to be fed with the true meat and drink of those who are mighty in spirit—which is the flesh and blood of His sacrifice. This comes as we are taught, by His grace, to count the world and all that is in it as nothing for the sake of knowing Him in His resurrection life. (See Philippians 3:10.)

Only the Lord Jesus is tender enough, in His love, to move so kindly within us that we become strong enough in Him, secure enough in Him, to stop this endless and tiresome battle to "save" and "protect" ourselves. Which we cannot do! So high and good is the love of Jesus, as He births us and nurtures us in this new life from heaven, that it cannot be said of anyone but Him—He is the true mother of all life and all that is godly and good. . . .

For is this not so? The kindest and most loving mother is the one who knows the greatest need of her child—not just the apparent outward need, but what is needed for the life of the child, which is within. She guards her child in body *and* in spirit. . . .

As the child grows, she will not continue to treat it as an infant or a child. She will teach it how to act in strength and understanding, according to its ability. She will act differently, but her love does not change. She allows the child to be chastised to destroy its faults—for in this way we understand our weaknesses, and are humbled so that we can receive virtues and grace. . . .

In all of this—from our spiritual birth to our growth in the nature of Christ—Jesus treats us with a tenderness that cannot be compared to any other. For our soul is so precious in His sight.

Love penetrates—for nothing but love can crack the hard shell of sin that encloses our spirit. And when love has come in, the seed is germinated. Then He is the spark of new, godly understanding. He prepares all our paths, as pathways of teaching and instruction. He pours His cleansing water over our conscience. He comforts our inner being. He illumines our mind with wisdom. . . . And when we fall, He quickly lifts us up in His loving embrace.

In this way, little by little, He strengthens us by His sweet working. So the love He has planted within us grows as we choose to walk in Christ, and it reaches full fruit, bursting out in sweet fragrance in all our words and actions.

So shall we grow in the power of grace, as His beloved children, forever and forever.

*F*ather of Grace, I know you must become hard toward me sometimes—the way a loving mother becomes firm in order to redirect the stubborn child.

Help me to quickly accept your correcting grace. Bring me back into the peace that flows from you like the comforting and unstoppable waters of a great river. . . .

31

He Knows Our Frailty

*Since [God's] children have flesh and blood, [Jesus] too
shared in their humanity. . . . He had to be made like his
brothers in every way, in order that he might become
a merciful and faithful high priest. . . . We do not have
a high priest who is unable to sympathize
with our weaknesses. . . .*

Hebrews 2:14, 17; 4:15

*If anybody does sin, we have one who speaks to the
Father in our defense—Jesus Christ,
the Righteous One.*

1 John 2:1

There are some people whom the Lord allows
to fall very hard, so that they are caused great grief.
In fact, some experience a fall worse than anything
they did before they were born into Christ.

When it happens to us, we think all of our growth in Christ up to that point is wasted. But we think this way only because we have a very small perspective. We do not see from God's higher viewpoint the deeper work He is about to do. It is not true that all our faithfulness and spiritual growth amount to nothing. And I am about to show you a wondrous mystery in the love of Christ.

Some of us *need* to fall—only God knows who, and it is not up to us to grant ourselves this license. But God knows that some of us, after a grievous fall, will be awakened to see how the operation of His grace works. For if we did not fall we would not see where we have depended upon our own strengths to help and to save us. And every human strength is puny—until it is brought within the mighty strength of God.

And if we did not fall, we would not have deeper insight into the amazing love of our Creator—how He knows our every weakness, how He works to turn our failings into glory and spiritual might. For one day, when we stand in heaven, we will look back on our falling and we will understand how terrible our sin really is— much worse than our pained conscience can know right now! But we will also see that no outward act of sin ever hurt us, no matter what the effects of sin were upon our outer man. We will see that His love never allowed us any spiritual harm, not if we allow sin to awaken us to our need for greater and greater dependence upon the Lord.

Yes, one day we will see that we were not valued less by the Lord, not even in our sin. . . . From everlasting to everlasting is the love that cannot be destroyed—*will not* be destroyed—by our foolish failures. . . !

When you are distressed, then, by your failures, do not run from the Lord—as if any of us could hide from Him! Instead, run to Him quickly . . . and say, "I have corrupted myself and made myself filthy, and I hate it because now I'm not like you. I cannot be clean again—I cannot be free from this corruption—unless you come and lift me and help me."

And He always comes. . . .

All-Wise Father, I praise you today for *Jesus . . . my Lord . . . my advocate . . . my brother.*

Thank you for understanding . . . helping . . . causing me to rise and walk free . . . even from the deadliest traps that are set for me.

32

He Lifts Us Up

Endure hardship . . . like a good soldier of Christ Jesus.

2 Timothy 2:3

Endure afflictions . . .

2 Timothy 4:5, KJV

I heard a loud voice from the throne, saying, ". . . God himself will wipe away every tear from [your] eyes. There will be no more death or mourning or crying or pain, for the old order of things has passed away."

Revelation 21:3–4

Once I was given these words:

I am leading you above. And one day you will come up above, where you will have me for your reward—a crown for your head! Then you will be filled from the wellspring of peace and everlasting happiness that flows from of old, and flows without end.

God tells us in His Word to fix our minds on

what is high and holy and pure. (See Philippians 4:8–9.) We do this in contemplation. He wants us to practice contemplation as often as possible, for as long as we can, as His grace gives us strength. I am referring to silent prayer in which we fix our soul on the invisible attributes of God—His goodness, love, and the like. This prayer fills us with the peace that comes from God, a serenity that is like experiencing the glory of heaven itself, while it lasts.

Yes, while it lasts. . . .

For we are prone to fall back into ourselves. This is the way it will be, as long as we are in these bodies—though we may fall into ourselves less and less as we practice contemplation, which is our means of walking with the Lord in His light.

We sometimes fall into ourselves through depression, or through persistent spiritual blindness that is our plague. We also suffer physical pains, as well as spiritual dryness, all because of our frail passing nature. In all these things which weigh down our soul, God longs for us to fix this firm fact in our mind—especially when our soul tells us otherwise: *He is present with us always. He never forgets us or leaves us. He continues to walk beside us, even though we have become blind to His face, numb to His touch.*

He is speaking to you now, and to me, with these words—by which He means to offer us bracing strength and tender comfort:

I am leading you to the place where there is no more

pain of any kind, in body or in spirit. Nothing there will make you sick, or displease your heart, or oppose your will. . . . You will look back from there and wonder why it should have afflicted you so to endure on earth. For it is my will, and endurance works to reveal my glory in you.

God wants us to embrace His commands, which come from love. Then we will know His consolation, too, which He gives generously. We do so by accepting the work of suffering—both the work it does in us, and the witness it is to others when He gives us patience and serene peace in suffering.

Having suffered terrible, terrible pain myself, I can only encourage you with this, which has helped me endure—and more than endure! Accept all pain as lightly as you are able. Do not focus your soul upon it and make it an even heavier load than it is. I make it my practice now to count pain as nothing. For the more lightly we accept our sorrows, and the less importance we give to them—*because we know we have His love*—the less pain will be able to hold us down

And in that day when we are fully risen, above everything, the greater will be our reward for overcoming.

My Father, time and eternity are in your hands!

I have your life and your power within this flesh. In you—strengthened by your love and power—I will do more than endure any affliction. In you I will overcome . . . from this day until the day you raise me to the life that is without end!

33

He Gives Us Victory

The LORD *says . . ."Sit at my right hand until I make your enemies a footstool for your feet." . . . [For] you will rule in the midst of your enemies.*

Psalm 110:1–2

Thanks be to God, who always leads us in triumphal procession in Christ and through us spreads everywhere the fragrance of the knowledge of him.

2 Corinthians 2:14

*I*t is God's will that you and I see ourselves bound to Christ in an indestructible oneness.

Personally, I have come to see myself as one with Christ. And everything which He has done—the work of salvation, the conquering of hell, and ascension to the right hand of God—has been done for me. My place is with Him.

So it is for everyone who is united with the heavenly Lover of souls. You and I can only understand this as our soul grows in the love that is planted in us. . . .

If we are hidden with Christ in God, then nothing anyone says or does can harm our eternal soul. Everything and everyone that God allows to come to us—and nothing comes except it is allowed—is permitted by love. This is the true and great salvation accomplished for us in Christ, and we are one with Him.

God reveals this so we can understand where our true home is, the only walls of strength that can protect us from harm. He is our soul's home, so that we will love Him, and run in to Him, and be safe. He wants us to take delight in Him, as He delights in us. He wants us only to reverence Him, for He is great and we have nothing outside of Him to fear.

And now I will show you another thing—for there are many Christians who carry an inordinate fear, not only of men but of the devil, too. They spend so much time worrying about him!

As I have told you, God wants us to know that all the evil might of the Enemy is shut up and contained inside the hand of our Friend. It is true: Our soul has nothing at all to fear from Satan.

Is this not what your soul has longed for—to be free from the terrible burden of worry and fear? We are free, then, for all the wickedness of men and the devil is under the power of the One we love . . . the One who loves us.

That is why I tell you, when you experience temptation, sickness, opposition, or loss . . . though it is real in this life . . . look upon it as nothing more than a bad dream you must endure while you are in this life, which is our soul's night. . . .

And God himself will give us the strength to continue walking with Christ in spirit . . . until the light of our soul's morning is come.

Father, Maker of lights and Light, I need this "indestructible oneness" with Christ. Set me free, today . . . from all worry and fear . . . from temptation and doubt.

Lord, as these dark weapons of the Enemy withdraw, your light pours over the hills into my soul. . . . You are my Morningstar!

34

He Is Our
Nobility

*"Fallen! Fallen is Babylon the Great! . . . Come out of
her my people, so that you will not share in her sins, so
that you will not receive any of her plagues. . . ." [Then
I saw] the Holy City . . . coming down out of heaven
from God. It shone with the glory of God. . . . Nothing
impure will ever enter it, nor will anyone who does
what is shameful or deceitful, but only those whose
names are written in the Lamb's book of life.*

Revelation 18:2, 4; 21:10–11, 27

*T*he Lord opened the eyes of my soul, and He
showed me another wondrous sight.

*I saw my soul in the midst of my being. My soul is as
wide as an endless fortress—a blessed kingdom. It is clean
and beautiful, and in it there exists a fine city.*

*In the center of that city sits our Lord Jesus. He is both
true God and true man. His being is radiant and handsome.
He is dressed in the vestments of the Shepherd of All
Souls—and in the garments of the Most High King. And*

He is wearing the banners of one who is greatly honored for
many mighty deeds.

As He sits there, regal and erect, He himself is the
uprightness of the whole city of the soul. As Prince of Peace,
He rules. As Lord of Sabbath Rest, He guards over heaven
and earth and all that exists. . . .

The place that Jesus has taken within the soul
He will never, never leave . . . and there is a reason
for this, which I will later show you. . . .

For now, you would do well to contemplate this
wondrous soul that is in you. For the Lord revealed
to me the delight He took in the creation of our soul.
As perfect as the Father could create a creature . . . as
perfect as the Son could create a creature . . . the
Holy Spirit in full agreement—so it was done. . . .

It remains for us to value our own soul, then—to
esteem it as much as the Lord and King who lives
within it. The creature must be led along to see the
great nobility of the Ruler, and the Ruler's dominion,
which is the marvelous soul of man. When the
creature sees how low is every lesser thing compared
to this Lord and His dominion, then in wonder it is
moved to seek above the things of this earth—to seek
for that high place where its Lord dwells.

In this way, the soul must be led to understand
it will find rest and peace and joy and life in *nothing*
here below . . . for all things here below are beneath
our soul's true dignity.

We are so greatly esteemed by God. . . .

Father—Maker of my soul, because you made me—you, and no other—I am raised and dignified. You breathe your presence, your Self, into me, and I am lifted and clothed with high esteem.

By your grace, Father, continue to press my soul and mold me into the image of your Son, Jesus . . . who waits in majesty to be Ruler of my whole being.

35
He Gives Spiritual Wisdom

The God of all grace, who called you to his eternal glory in Christ . . . will himself . . . make you strong, firm and steadfast.

1 Peter 5:10

You who are trying to be justified by law have been alienated from Christ; you have fallen away from grace. But by faith we eagerly await through the Spirit the righteousness for which we hope. . . . The only thing that counts is faith expressing itself through love.

Galatians 5:4–6

The Lord wishes us to continue on in our pilgrim's journey in faith—fixing before us the City of God, where Jesus rules, as our one goal. The Lord wants to abide with us as we move along on this journey, all the way to the end of our lives.

137

And this is accomplished in us as we press on in the faith.

Trust, then, in all His promises. Know that He is only good—issuing every goodness to us.

How urgent it is for us to keep building ourselves in the faith, and to encourage one another. For our soul has many enemies and faces opposition on every side as it walks the narrow way of faith.

We must make our way through the pitfalls of our blind spots.

We are called astray by spiritual enemies of the cross, the enemies of Christ—whether they are knowing or unknowing in their opposition to Him. And these enemies exist *within us*, as well as in the outward world of men and women we face every day.

That is why I tell you to practice the inward contemplation that always opens our sight to our precious Lover. Then He shines the light of His wisdom upon our path—that is, the wisdom of Jesus himself, who is the living Word. It is this light of His presence which we need to truly teach us, so that we know from within the true instruction of God. It is the light of His wisdom by which we learn to separate the living Word of God—the law of love and of grace—from the teachings of men who still have only earthly and legalistic understanding.

No matter how the Lord chooses to instruct our soul—whether by His Spirit from within, or by men who are wise in the things of the Spirit—it is all meant so that we perceive Him wisely. We must learn to do this so that we do not fall back into a lower mind that is subject to the law but continue to grow in the light of grace.

Faith, mixed with grace—this is what keeps us in Christ Jesus. Nothing remains between the soul and its heavenly Maker when we continue to walk in this way, in godly wisdom. For then nothing at all can hinder us from going boldly to Him. I warn you, anything less than this kind of spiritual faith is nothing but law. And the law can never bring health or life to the soul.

In the faith—I mean, a spiritual faith—this is where the Lord wants us to keep our souls. Because of His sweet love for us, because of His merciful actions in Christ, we ought to oblige Him by continuing in the one true path He asks us to walk. . . .

*M*y *Father, so often I have one law for me—I want lenience and kindness. And I have another law for others—I want justice, payment, apologies.*

Give me your love and grace so I can rule consistently over all I do and say.

36

He Is Our Path

"God is mighty . . . and firm in his purpose. . . . He
does not take his eyes off the righteous. . . ."

Job 36:5, 7

[And] we see Jesus, who was made a little lower than
the angels, now crowned with glory and honor because
he suffered death, so that by the grace of God
he might taste death for everyone.

Hebrews 2:9

I have told you several times you would do
well to cultivate the practice of contemplation—for
by it your soul will greatly benefit. And you will
receive strength in your inner man, no matter what
befalls you on your spiritual journey into God.

Therefore, I will show you three means of
contemplation—three paths which will never fail to
lead you to the spiritual wellspring that issues
health and strength to your soul—and you *will* find
health if you make it a practice to fix these things

before you and do not simply agree they are good things to think about.

The first is the suffering of our Lord. For when He was with us in this life, He revealed himself as fully man. He was tempted in all things as we are. He experienced every kind of anguish we can feel. Remember that He went so far in His obedience to God He willingly suffered a criminal's bitter death, which was God's will, though the punishment was so unjust because He himself had done no wrong.

You will know when you have comprehended the truths in this contemplation—for your soul will first experience tremendous sorrow and grief. That is because you will be given full understanding that God died in your place, for your errors.

The second path of contemplation begins as you fix your soul upon our heavenly Lover.

When we comprehend the truth of the love of Christ, we will never be shaken from the knowledge that His love is unfailing. We will understand His tender pity, for He knows our weak frame. And we will be touched to the core by His compassion, by which He ever walks at our side to rescue us in all our falling. We will be driven to our knees in utter humility when we are led to full understanding that the One we have scorned, rejected, and sent out to His death—He is none other than our Lover, and the only One who really loves us.

The third path of contemplation I will recommend begins as you set your soul upon the high, noble nature of the Lord as He reigns in state within your soul.

When the truths of His rule and reign are revealed to us, our soul will be founded upon an unshakable trust. For we will see Him as He is— God from everlasting to everlasting, containing all that is created in himself, Sovereign over everything that comes into our lives. . . .

If you are faithful in these contemplations, laboring to bring your wayward soul into the rest that is in Christ (Hebrews 4–6), I assure you of this. A sweet light will fall upon your soul, and the light of the Spirit's life and wisdom will begin to guide you.

This is the way of faith. It will lead us to our one Hope, our one Love. It will break our hearts with proper godly sorrow when we sin. It will renew our soul's devotion to Christ—who is the true path. In this way, we remain in the comforting presence of the Lord.

It is a sure means of keeping our soul open to the inner working of grace, which is the power of our Lord God to fill us with everlasting life.

My Father, thank you for watching over my soul and fulfilling your purpose for me in this life.

In this moment, I set my eyes on Christ, considering the path He walked . . . descending through ranks of worshiping angels, to suffer and serve on earth . . . to raise me. . . .

What is my path today, Father?

37
He Keeps Us From Danger

*Live as free men, but do not use your freedom as a
cover-up for evil. . . . [Jesus] himself bore our sins in his
body on the tree, so that we might die to sins
and live for righteousness; by his wounds
you have been healed.*

1 Peter 2:16, 24

And now I must warn you of a deadly danger.

I am hoping by now you have understood the
way of life, the way of grace that is in Christ—who
is the beginning and the end of all things for us.
And I hope you understand now what it means to
be "in Christ."

With this understanding, I will now tell you
how deadly sin is in creatures—deadly, I say, even
to those who are not destined to die for sin but to
live forever in the endless joy of God. Consider
seriously what I am about to say.

The two greatest opposing forces that exist are

these—the high joy that flows down to us from above, and the terrible abyss of anguish that lies hidden in the darkness of sin. The highest joy of all is to possess the Father—till there remains no shred of darkness nor cloud nor even a mist between us and His endless pure light. The highest joy is to see Him as He is, to feel all the sweetness of His being nourishing our soul, rejoined to Him in our very substance.

Once I was shown the smallest part of what this union will be like.

I saw that the only thing that blocks us from living in the rays of God's pure light now is sin: first, our hunger for sin; then the action of sin itself; finally, the wasting starvation sin causes to our souls. For such empty darkness can never feed our souls, which were made for endless light. (As I told you before, sin is empty—it is nothing at all.)

This is why we blind men and women must be reminded, over and over again, that when we pursue sin its only fruit will be wasting sickness to our soul. Then comes starvation, which eventually causes blindness.

Do you see the tragedy in this?

Sin, which is nothing, becomes thick as a wall of darkness—a wall built right within us—imprisoning us and keeping us from the freedom that is ours in Him who is Light. And the more we pursue sin, the more we cause the wall of darkness to be built around our soul, the house of our inner man. And the more horrible our sins, the more we turn and flee from the light. Sin makes us like the brute beast who, when injured, thrashes and flees in terror from the kindest husbandman who has only come to its rescue.

Sin, I tell you, strikes the soul with wounds. And in the way I was shown, the wounds become mortal as the light of God—which is our soul's life—drains out. Until the soul can do the most hideous crimes and wickedness against its fellow creatures and not feel the slightest pang of conscience. by which we are awakened. That is why sin puts our soul always in danger of death—why the first small part of the soul enters in to a little corner of hell itself.

Do you now see the path sin puts you on? And if you know this now, how can you ever pursue even the slightest sin ever again?

For all the time we are pursuing sin we are running after death. Remember that sin is this: to look for the spiritual food that re-creates your soul—that is, love and life and beauty and truth—in any created creature or thing. When we pursue our life in anything other than God, our soul becomes weak and failing. And if we are not careful, the eyes of our soul will close and become dead and dried. In this way, a man or woman can rot from within, and die, and yet think they live. What a great tragedy! For then they cannot see Him who is our blessed Life.

This is why I have told you, and why the holy Church says in its teaching, that sin is devious and strikes mortal blows to your soul.

My Father, *you who rescue me from danger, there are people I know—people I love—who are wandering in sin away from you. By my life, Lord, and by your words through me . . . call them out of darkness.*

Send me humbly to someone whom you are calling to your great wedding feast . . . someone who does not even know they are invited.

146

38

He Smiles

*You are all [children] of the light and . . . of the day.
We do not belong to the night or to the darkness. So
then, let us not be like others, who are asleep. . . . But
since we belong to the day, let us be self-controlled,
putting on faith and love as a breastplate, and the hope
of salvation as a helmet. For God did not appoint us
to suffer wrath. . . .*

1 Thessalonians 5:5–6, 8–9, KJV

In everything I was shown about sin, which I
have shown you, I saw a truth more wonderful—
which made my own soul leap.

God does not see us as horrifying dead things,
corrupted in our trespasses and sins. Nor does He
ever depart from us. . . . Remember that to flee from
corruption is a law that was given to our flesh. For
the law was the schoolmaster of our fleshly outer
man, to teach us to flee from sin in the inward man.
The law was given to drive us to God until full
grace was revealed—and grace is none other than
the life now opened to us in Christ! (See Romans
3:20.)

Yes, I saw how looking for our life in everything that is not Life is deadly to us for a little while. Like eating the tiniest bit of poison every day. But we are creatures destined for the Light that has no beginning or end!

Then turn from lesser pursuits! Turn from all your small, poisoning darknesses to face the endless Light!

Let the river of grace spread God's love far and wide, high and deep in your soul. For love is first, and love is what draws us to the Light. So we are drawn, and we step a little further into the Light— and then we see, first only the vaguest outlines of something. What is it? *A face.* We fear. It was sin that made us fear. Then we timidly step forward into greater light, and we see that the face is not angry, though we were so sure it was angry. But our soul sees the expression of pleasure—great pleasure that we have returned from our walk in the wilderness of darkness. And in this walk in spirit, we are coaxed more and more out of darkness into Light. And the more we walk in the Light, the more we will hunger for our soul's true and only food—the food that is from heaven. Until we come to ache with a longing, the lover's hunger for the Beloved.

We become desperate in our need to love. For as we peer through the fleeting mists of this life and peer into the light of love, we see emerging the form and image of God's own likeness. . . . Then we are no longer shut up in our dark and selfish hell but are free to run to him as children at play in the Light, needing only one thing for our soul's assurance and peace and well-being—until we receive our soul's reward and prize, which is nothing else than a full and open look into Love's true face.

Yes, it is true our Lord dwells with us now. He is in us, here present, embracing us and enclosing us in himself, never to leave us, nearer than we can say in failing human words. Yet our soul will never cease from mourning, from this journey of seeking and longing, until that day when we emerge fully into Light and behold Him fully . . . and feel His embrace, with our face pressed against the face of our Lord.

In that moment, even the tiniest wisp of sadness will vanish in His risen light. . . .

My Father, King of Heaven, you call me "son of the light." You crown my head with the knowledge of you and of your way of life.

You call me "son of the day," and you promise to wake me to the day that will not end . . . eternal life!

For a moment, I will push aside all regret, all sadness . . . to be touched and renewed by the rays of your goodness. . . .

39
He Embraces

The path of the righteous is like the first gleam of dawn, shining ever brighter till the full light of day.

Proverbs 4:18

"My lover is mine and I am his . . . until the day breaks and the shadows flee. . . ."

Song of Songs 2:16–17

I want you to think on what I am about to tell you—to consider it deeply, until the truth of it breaks like the ray of dawn, cresting over hills to shine within you. Wait, I say, until Dayspring rises in you.

He who is all your joy is near to you right now—in this moment. He could not be closer if He were holding you, pressing you to himself, your two faces touching. It is the embrace of the Spirit, as the Beloved draws you into himself.

When I saw this, my own heart broke . . . and I laughed and wept at the same time—laughed with delight, and wept with unspeakable mourning at our predicament.

Because of His high and surpassing goodness, He keeps us so close! And it is all because of our persistent blindness and ignorance that we go on resisting Him, trying to pull away and flee from the embrace of the One who is only Life. O wretched, hateful blindness!

How long must we bear the weight of this cloak of mortality, this leaden soul that drags us from our Love's embrace? How long must we stumble in the darkness of these fleshly eyes, bruising and bloodying our souls as we grope for Life . . . cutting our tender souls against hard-edged death?

. . . I sit in mourning and pity for my own soul's tremendous loss. And no words can express the pain I feel when I understand the stupidity of my own unbelief. How is it possible I will always be prone to forget the truth I have seen when He holds me in His Light? He longs to hold me in endless love and faithfulness . . . until the day when this pathetic flesh ceases to drag me from His arms. . . .

Now it is only in the blessed vision of Him I find an end to my soul's grief and longing. For He has touched me, and outside of Him I can never be free from these pains—which are the pangs of love. . . .

My Father, by the light of your righteousness I see the path of life!

By your Word, by your example in Christ, by your Spirit . . . help me to speak, and act, and show your heart . . . to the people you have placed in my path . . . people you care for.

Help me to be faithful . . . until the dawn breaks.

40
Our Feast Is Prepared

In that day, the LORD Almighty will be a glorious crown . . . for his people.

Isaiah 28:5

Blessed is the man who perseveres . . . because when he has stood the test, he will receive the crown of life that God has promised to those who love him.

James 1:12

I promised before I would reveal something to you about the dwelling of God that is within you. And now I shall. . . .

In one of the showings, which our gracious Lord granted to me, this was shown to me:

When the manservant stood before his regal lord, dressed in ragged clothing to do his lord's will, I saw that the lord was not seated in some splendid palace, on a throne.

No, he was sitting on the ground in a barren place—alone in a wilderness wasteland.

The lord's robes were of a billowing and clear azure blue . . . by which I knew that all the heavens were contained in him. He was most dignified—and more beautiful than I can tell. By his whole demeanor, mercy poured from him. . . .

His eyes were deep with loving pity . . . so I knew that within him lay my palace of refuge, my only place of security, as if in him there is a palace long and wide and full as heaven itself.

And I saw that the same loving attentiveness the lord had for his manservant—even when the servant fell and was wretched and alone—this same utter attentiveness he has for us. It was something in the tender look of love within the lord's eyes. . . .

If you could behold it, it would melt your hard heart, and with your resistant soul, your heart would split open to Him for joy! . . .

And I saw the servant leave for a time to toil in the lord's garden—to toil until the seeds he plants in many, many souls split open and grow. And what is it that he is growing? I saw that it is a sweet fruit, a rare fruit he was sent out to prepare for his lord . . . a special fruit that is all to his lord's liking! And he will never leave his work until the day he is ready to present the full fruit of all his labors to his lord. . . .

And I saw that day! The servant comes before his lord again. He is no longer dressed in our rags, but is arrayed in pure white splendor. He comes to present the food that is the feast of his lord . . . and returns to the same place where he left his lord, seated on the ground in a wasteland. . . .

But I saw that the wilderness is not at all the same place *he left. As he returns bearing his fruit, the wilderness is suddenly transformed into a place of thrones, and a Heaven of heavens. . . .*

And the Son now stands before His Father, richly revealed in the white robes of His wedding. And the feast is prepared. And the mystery of our iniquity and our leaving is revealed for a moment . . . to be swallowed up and destroyed along with our death, in endless love and light.

Then I saw this, which felled the soul within me, so that even now I drop to my knees in silent awe and wonder.

For the Father presents the Son to us. And the Son is our crown! And the Father presents us to the Son. And we are His crown!

So all the joy of heaven began to toll. And together with the Son, we will turn to face the Father as one. And then is the work of the Father, His highest and crowning work, complete. And the Father's heart breaks open with joy in that hour . . . pouring out all the marvels of re-created heaven and earth. . . .

. . . which will be our endless bliss, mine and yours and all who will be saved in the Son . . . a heaven of joy which is now our home forever!

Father, keep me true and tender to Jesus, who is Lord of the Feast.

Let the heaven of your presence grow within me, today

and every day until my journey here is complete . . . and I stand before you in the Son . . . and the wedding feast begins. . . .

. . . and I receive the promised crown of life!

DAVID HAZARD developed the REKINDLING THE INNER FIRE devotional series to encourage others to keep the "heart" of their faith alive and afire with love for God. He also feels a special need to help Christians of today to "meet" men and women of the past whose experience of God belongs to the whole Church, for all the ages.

Hazard is an award-winning writer, the author of books for both adults and children, with international bestsellers among his many titles. He lives in northern Virginia with his wife, MaryLynne, and three children: Aaron, Joel, and Sarah Beth.